Street by Street

C000017946

OXFORD

ABINGDON, KIDLINGTON, WITNEY

Botley, Drayton, Eynsham, Headington, Kennington, Long Hanborough, Marcham, Wheatley, Woodstock, Yarnton

2nd edition September 2004
© Automobile Association Developments Limited 2006

Original edition printed May 2001

Ordnance Survey® This product includes map data licensed from Ordnance Survey® with the permission of the Controller of Her Majesty's Stationery Office. © Crown copyright 2006. All rights reserved. Licence number 399221.

Published by AA Publishing (a trading name of Automobile Association Developments Limited, whose registered office is Fanum House, Basing View, Basingstoke, Hampshire RG21 4EA. Registered number 1878835).

Mapping produced by the Cartography Department of The Automobile Association. (A02969)

A CIP Catalogue record for this book is available from the British Library.

Printed by GRAFIASA S.A., Porto, Portugal

The contents of this atlas are believed to be correct at the time of the latest revision. However, the publishers cannot be held responsible or liable for any loss or damage occasioned to any person acting or refraining from action as a result of any use or reliance on any material in this atlas, nor for any errors, omissions or changes in such material. This does not affect your statutory rights. The publishers would welcome information to correct any errors or omissions and to keep this atlas up to date. Please write to Publishing, The Automobile Association, Fanum House (FH12), Basing View, Basingstoke, Hampshire, RG21 4EA.

Ref: ML093z

Key to map pages	ii-iii
Key to map symbols	iv-1
Enlarged map pages	2-3
Main map pages	4-65
Index – towns & villages	66
Index – streets	67-71
Index – featured places	72-73
Acknowledgements	73

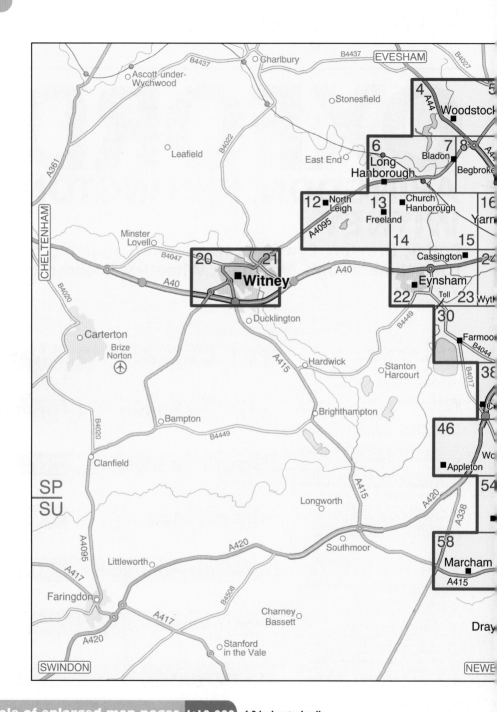

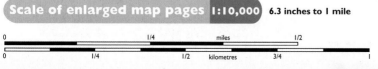

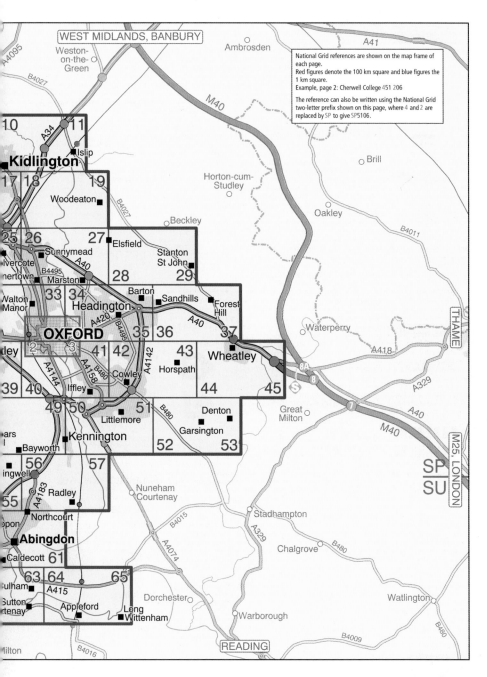

National Grid references are shown on the map frame of each page.
Red figures denote the 100 km square and blue figures the 1 km square.
Example, page 2: Cherwell College 451 206

The reference can also be written using the National Grid two-letter prefix shown on this page, where 4 and 2 are replaced by SP to give SP5106.

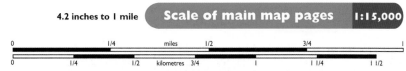

4.2 inches to 1 mile **Scale of main map pages** 1:15,000

iv

Junction 9	Motorway & junction	⊖	Underground station
Services	Motorway service area	⊖	Light railway & station
	Primary road single/dual carriageway	+++++++++	Preserved private railway
Services	Primary road service area	LC	Level crossing
	A road single/dual carriageway	•—•—•—•—•	Tramway
	B road single/dual carriageway	-----------	Ferry route
	Other road single/dual carriageway	....	Airport runway
	Minor/private road, access may be restricted	— · — · — · —	County, administrative boundary
← ←	One-way street	ʸʸʸʸʸʸʸʸ	Mounds
	Pedestrian area	17	Page continuation 1:15,000
------------	Track or footpath	3	Page continuation to enlarged scale 1:10,000
	Road under construction		River/canal, lake
[- - - -]	Road tunnel		Aqueduct, lock, weir
AA	AA Service Centre	465 ▲ Winter Hill	Peak (with height in metres)
P	Parking		Beach
P+	Park & Ride		Woodland
	Bus/coach station		Park
	Railway & main railway station		Cemetery
	Railway & minor railway station		Built-up area

	Featured building		Abbey, cathedral or priory
	City wall		Castle
A&E	Hospital with 24-hour A&E department		Historic house or building
PO	Post Office	Wakehurst Place NT	National Trust property
	Public library		Museum or art gallery
i	Tourist Information Centre		Roman antiquity
i	Seasonal Tourist Information Centre		Ancient site, battlefield or monument
	Petrol station, 24-hour Major suppliers only		Industrial interest
†	Church/chapel		Garden
	Public toilets		Garden Centre Garden Centre Association Member
	Toilet with disabled facilities		Garden Centre Wyevale Garden Centre
PH	Public house AA recommended		Farm or animal centre
	Restaurant AA inspected		Zoological or wildlife collection
Madeira Hotel	Hotel AA inspected		Bird collection
	Theatre or performing arts centre		Nature reserve
	Cinema		Aquarium
	Golf course	V	Visitor or heritage centre
▲	Camping AA inspected		Country park
	Caravan site AA inspected		Cave
	Camping & caravan site AA inspected		Windmill
	Theme park		Distillery, brewery or vineyard

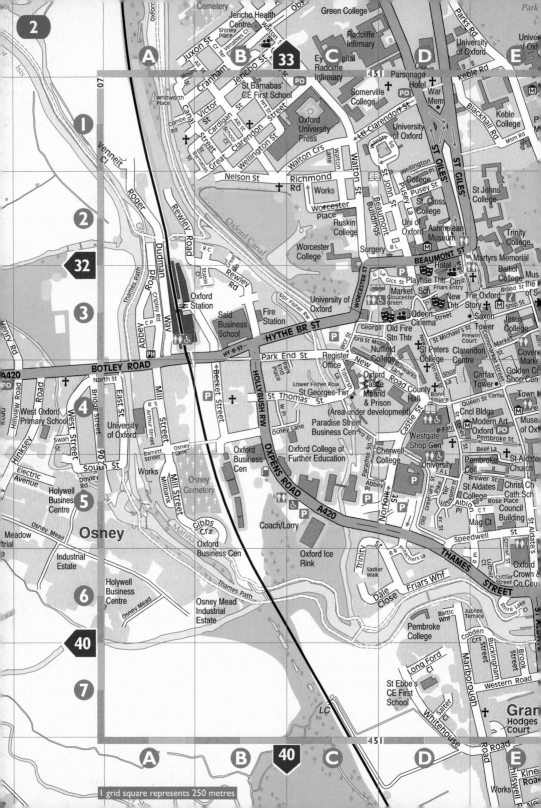

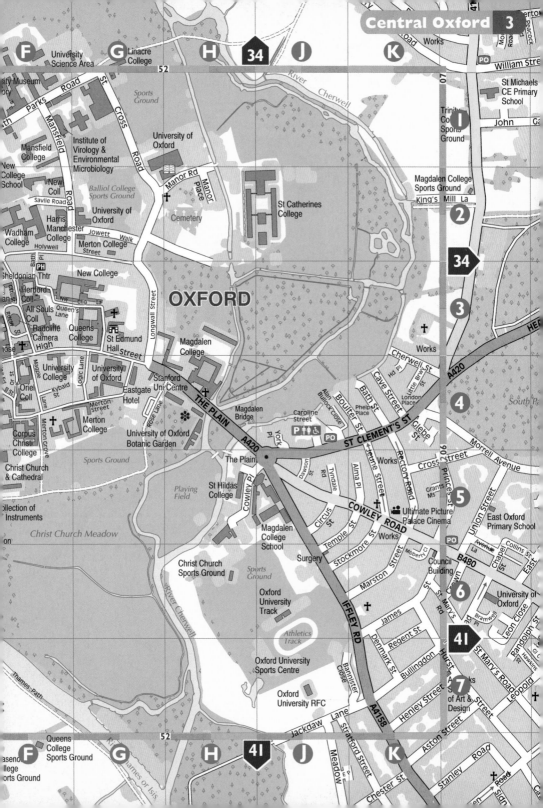

F
University Science Area

G
Linacre College

H

34

J

K
Works

St Michaels CE Primary School

John Ga

William Stre

PO

52

River Cherwell

Trinity Co Sports Ground

I

sity Museum
ory

Parks Road

Cross Road

Mansfield Road

St

Institute of Virology & Environmental Microbiology

University of Oxford

Manor Rd

Manor Place

Magdalen College Sports Ground

King's Mill La

2

Mansfield College

New College School

New Coll

Savile Road

Balliol College Sports Ground

University of Oxford

Cemetery

St Catherines College

34

Harris Manchester College

Wadham College

Holywell

Jowett Walk

Merton College Street

Works

3

Sheldonian Thtr

Bath

PH

New College

Longwall Street

OXFORD

Cherwell St

Hd Pl

A420

HEA

Hertford Coll

All Souls Coll

Radcliffe Camera

Queens College

Queen's Lane

St Edmund Hall

Magdalen College

Little Brw

London Place

Cave Street

South P

High

St Edmund Hall Street

Works

4

University College

Logic Lane

University of Oxford

Stanford Uni Centre

Magdalen Bridge

Caroline Street

Alan Bullock Close

Phelps Place

Boulter St

Bath St

Glebe St

Morrell Avenue

Oriel Coll

Kybald St

Merton Street

Eastgate Hotel

Rose Lane

The Plain

A420

York Pl

P

PO

ST CLEMENT'S ST

Rectory Road

Cross Street

Princes Street

Union Street

Corpus Christi College

Merton College

University of Oxford Botanic Garden

Dawson St

Tyndale Rd

Alma Pl

Jeune Street

Works

Grants MS

5

East Oxford Primary School

Christ Church & Cathedral

Sports Ground

The Plain

Cowley Pl

St Hildas College

Circus St

Temple St

Ultimate Picture Palace Cinema

COWLEY ROAD

Moberly Cl

PO

Avenue La

Collins St

Chapel St

East

collection of Instruments

Playing Field

Magdalen College School

Surgery

Stockmore St

Works

Council Building

B480

6

University of Oxford

on

Christ Church Meadow

River Cherwell

Christ Church Sports Ground

Sports Ground

IFFLEY RD

Marston St

James St

Leon Close

Bramwell

University of

Oxford University Track

Regent St

St Mary's Rd

Hurst St

41

Thames Path

Athletics Track

Denmark St

Bullingdon Rd

St Mary's Road

7

Oxford University Sports Centre

Bannister Close

Henley Street

of Art & Design

Oxford University RFC

A4158

Leopold

Jackdaw Lane

Stratford Street

Meadow

Aston Street

Stanley Road

Road

Queens College Sports Ground

seno lle

rounds

F

G

H

41

J

K

Chester St

52

Weaveley
Farms

E   F B4027   G   A4260   H

46   47

B4027

I

8

2

Banbury Road

BANBURY ROAD

A4095

Shipton Slade
Farm

3

ROAD

4

Banbury Road   Budds
Cl

Hensington

Hensington
Close

Marlborough
School   Woodstock
Swimming Pool

Woodstock
CE Primary School

Recreation
Rd

bury

CK

Cls Cl

Plane Tree
Wy

Briar
Ticket

Flemings Road

Glovers Cl

the Ley

Ride

rces

WK

Hedge
End

Shipton Road

CAMPSFIELD

Upper Campsfield
Farm

5

ercy
Covert

Churchill Gr

OXFORD

ROAD

A44

UPPER

46   47   216

E   A44   F   8   G A4095   H

6

Stonesfield Rd   Akeman

Combe

A   Park Road   **B**   **C**   **D**

Chatterpie Lane

4 4 1

9 1

Orchard Ct

Combe Gate

West End

Church Wk

Robin Hill

PO

Combe CE
Primary School

1

**East
End**

Bolton's Lane

2

4 5

Combe
Station

Mill
Wood

River Evenlode

3

Millwood

Millwood
Farm

End

Swan Lane

Bolsover Cl

Bk Wt Abelwood

Evenlode
Dr

Road

Myrtle
Close

Park Lane

**Long
Hanborough**

A4

4

WITNEY ROAD

A40

Slatters Ct

Hurdeswell

Hurdeswell

New
Road

MAIN RD.

Wastie's
Orch

Surgery

MAIN ROAD

Manor
House

PO

Rley Cl

Hanborough
Manor CE
School

2

Clyme Way

Roosevelt
Rd

Pinsley Rd

Marlborough Crs

Churchill Wy

Isis Cl

5

oslyn Road
ustrial

Wroslyn Road

Cooks Corner
Farm

Church Road

Pinsle
Woo

4 4 1

A   **13**   **B**   **C**   **D**

Freeland

Oakland
Close

Freeland

PO

Park

1 grid square represents 500 metres

E F G H

Blenheim
Palace

4

The
Lake

Lower Park

I

44 45

GROVE ROAD

The
Homestead

2

A4095

River Glyne

Park Lane

Park Cl

Park La

Bladon

PO

Bladon CE
Primary School

The
Lince

3

Church St

8

A4095 PARK STREET

Lamb Lane

Manor Rd

Heath Lane

MAIN ROAD

Hanborough
Business Park

Lodge Rd

Bankside

Fenlock Rd

Lower Road

4

Hanborough
Station

Oxford Bus
Museum

M

214

Bladon
Heath

5

Mill
Farm

44 45

Burleigh
Wood

E F G H

15

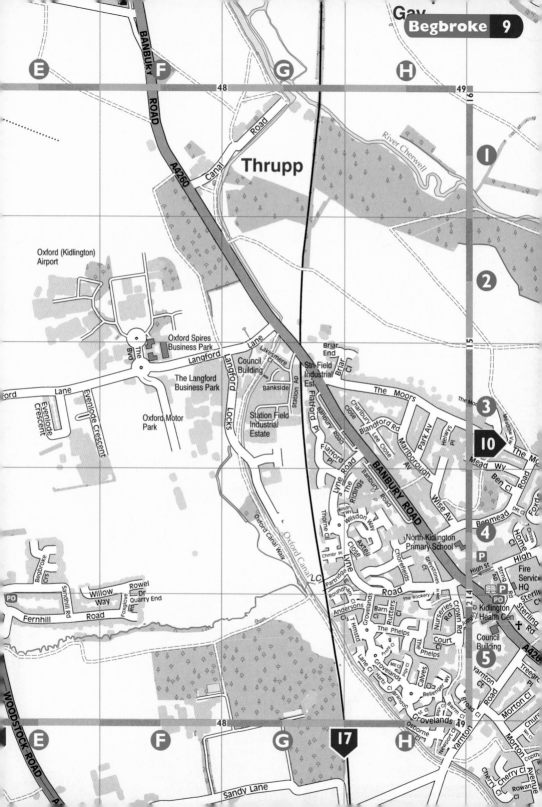

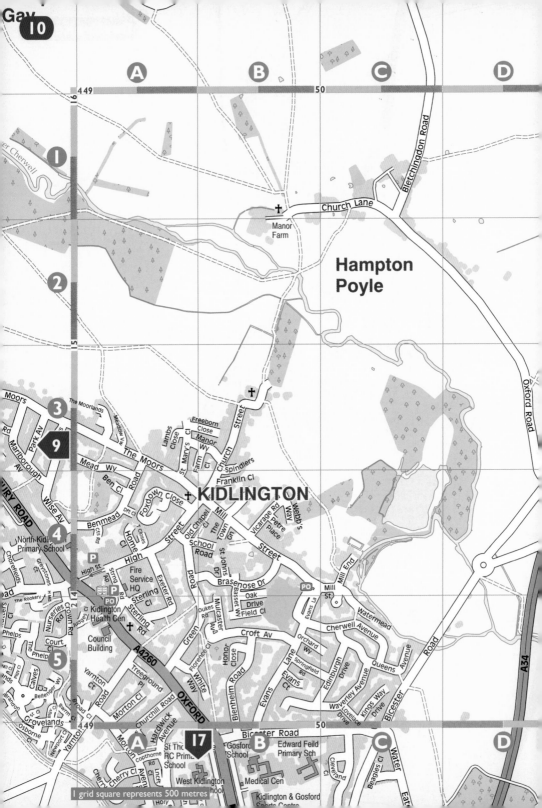

E   F   G   A34   H

52   53   16

1

Hampton
Gorse

Chipping
Farm

Br
Fa

Field Barn
Farm

B4027

2

15

BLETCHINGDON

3

Oxfordshire Way

ROAD

Islip
Station
Conyger
Close

Surgery

Cr Cl

Dr Souths
CE Primary
School

North St

Hilton
Gdns

4

Kidlington
Road

Church
Close

HIGH ST

Middle

KW

Islip

Church Lane

North Walk

Middle Street

Lower Street

214

The Rise

KING'S HEAD LA

THE HK

LC

Mill Farm

MILL

Street

Collice
Street

Bridge St

WHEATLEY ROAD

5

E   F   G   H

52   19   53

Northfield   BA

Oxford

12

North Leigh

Boddington Lane

Field Farm

A   B   C   D

438   39

Perrotts Hill Farm

North Leigh Business Park

Nursery Rd

A4095

North Leigh FC

Green Lane

New Yatt Road

Bridewell Cl

Church Road

Kn H

Perrott Close

Comm La

Evenlode Cl

Windmill Hts

PO

Windmill Close

Road

Cmmn Cl

Common Road

Leigh Cl

North Leigh CE Primary School

Park Road

Windmill Road

Wilcote VW

Park Cl

WS

Parkside

Lady Well Cl

Road

A4095

Osney Hill Farm

Eynsham Hall

Scotts House School & Da Nursery

Eynsham Park

95

438   39

A OX29   B   C   D

Cogges Wood

1 grid square represents 500 metres

E

Wroslyn Road Industrial Est

F

Cooks Corner Farm

G

6

H

Wroslyn Road

I

Freeland

Oakland Close

Freeland CE Primary School

Parklands

PO

Woodlands

Church View

The Blowings

Nash La

Hurst La

Broad Marsh La

Busby Cl

Walkers Cl

Blenheim Lane

Pigeon

2

use

Broad Marsh La

Websters Close

Wroslyn Road

Cuckoo Lane

3

14

12

Wroslyn Road

4

Cuckoo Lane

Bowles Farm

Little Green Farm

5

41

42

2 11

E

F

G

H

Church Road

A

Barnard Gate

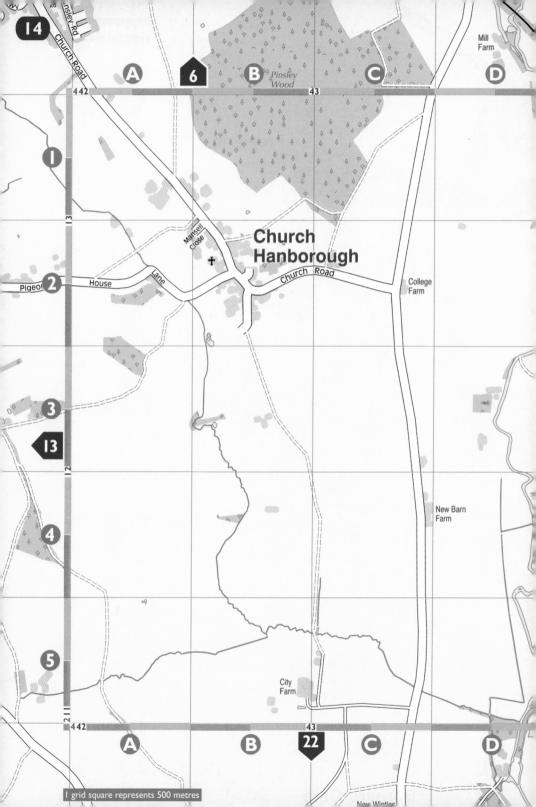

14

Church Road

A
6
B
Pinsley Wood
C
D
Mill Farm

442
43

1

13

Mansell Close

Church Hanborough

Lane

Pigeot
2
House
Church Road
College Farm

3

13

12

New Barn Farm

4

5

City Farm

211
442
43

A
B
22
C
D

New Wintles

1 grid square represents 500 metres

E *Burleigh Wood*

F

G

8

H

45

46

1

13

2

3

16

12

4

Burleigh Farm

Purwell Farm

Jericho Barns

W

5

211

E

F

23

45

G

46

H

Yarnton Road

Elms Road

The Green

Tennis

Bell

Bell Cl

od Cl

Lynton Lane

PO

St Peters CE (A) Primary School

St Peter's

La

16

A **8** B C D

4 46 47 WOODSTOCK ROAD A44

1

13

Farm
Spring Hill Road

Begbroke Wood

Stanley Cl

Broad Field

Ryle Rd

2

Spring Hill

Gravel Pit Lane

WOODSTOCK

Yarnton

The Spears
Willow Cl
Rutten
Aysgarth Road
Field Cl

Yarnton House

William Fletcher Primary School

The Garth

PO

3

15

12

Council Building

Stoutsfield Close

Little Blenheim

Bartholomew
Fletcher Close
Lane
Spencer Av
Dashwood Av
Merton Way

The Paddocks

Pound
St Tr Cl

4

Jericho Barns

Cassington Road

Park Cl

Church Lane

Worton

Yarnton Road

5

2 11

4 46 47

A B **24** C D

Tlane

1 grid square represents 500 metres

E F G **10** H

Council Building

Court
The Phelps

Calves
grovelands
Bellenger Wy

Yarnton
Ct

Yarnton
Road

Treeground
Pl

A4260

Whi

Honor
Close

Croft Av

Blenheim Road

Evans
Ct

Edinbu

Waverley Avenue

Kings Rd

Lovelace
Drive

Grovelands
Osborne
Newport Dr

Yarnton
49

Churchill Road

Hardwick

Avenue

Morton

ROAD

Bicester Road

50

St Thomas More
RC Primary
School

Gosford Hill
School

Edward Feild
Primary Sch

Medical Cen

Cleve

Cromwell Way

Beadles Av

I

LC

Cherry Cl

Cherry Cl

Copthorne

Rd

Lnct

Rowan
Cl

Spruce
Rd

Holly

West Kidlington
Primary School

Ash

Maple

Mgn Cl

Rd

Hwrtm Wy

Morton
Avenue

Avenue

ROAD

Kidlington & Gosford
Sports Centre

Gosford

Thames Valley
Police HQ

13

I

Yarnton Lane

Almond Av

Azalea Av

Laburnum
Crs

Hazel

Beech Crs

Lock Crs

Stratfield Rd

Elm
Gv

Crescent

Cromwell
Way

Fairfax Rd

Gosford
Close

Hampden

Drive

Astley Av

2

LC

Croxford
Gardens

South Avenue

South
Close

The
Broadway

PO

Superstore

Croxford Gdns

Stratfield
Farm

Stonehouse
Farm

WOODSTOCK

ROAD

A44

Oxford Canal Walk

Gosford
All Blacks
RFC

A4260

FRIEZE

WAY

A34

3

18

12

A4165

OXFORD

ROAD

A34

P+

4

Msh Cl

Cl Road

Bernard

Mead
Rd

ssington Road

Frieze
Farm

Golf Course

5

Oxford Canal Walk

Oxford Canal

Peartree
Hill

WOODSTOCK

RD

Holiday
Inn

luxkeside

211

North Oxfo
Golf Club

xey
lead

E F **25** G

49

Travelodge

Services

H

Linkside

50

Jordan

Jordan Hill
Business Park

A44

P+

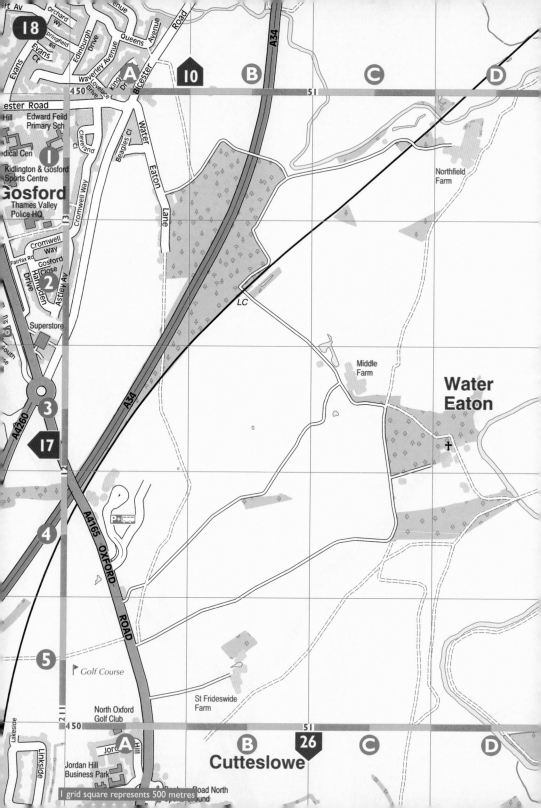

E **II** F G H

Mill

Street
Bridge St

LA WHEATLEY ROAD 53

Oxfordshire Way

B4027

I

Oxfordshire Way

3

2

Prattle
Wood

River Cherwell

3 B4027

Home
Farm

Woodeaton
Manor
School

12

Woodeaton

4

5

Woodeaton
Wood

2 II

E F **27** G H

53 54

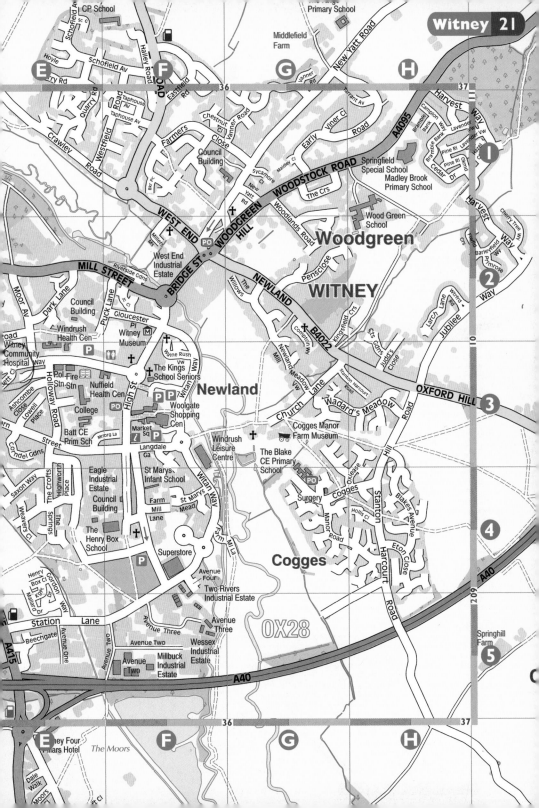

E   F   15   G   H

45   46

I

The Green

Yarnton Road

Elms Road

The Tennis

Bell Road

Lynton Lane

PO

od Cl   Bell Cl

St Peters CE (A) Primary School

St Peter's Cl

Cassington

Hollow Furlong

Church Lane

Pound Lane

Horsemere Lane

Manor Cl

Eynsham Road

Marlborough Drive

A40

40

2

0

3

24

4

River Thames or Isis

Wytham Great Wood

209

5

A44 OXFORD ROAD

Thames Path

Swinford Bridge (Toll)

E   **Swinford** 30   G   H

45   46

The Five

24

A   B   16   C   D

4 46   47

1

A40

2   River Thames or Isis

Thames Path

Thames Path

3

23

4

ytham
eat
ood

5

Wytha

PO

PH
†

A   B   31   C   D

4 46   47

1 grid square represents 500 metres

Wytham
Park

E   F   19   G   H

53   54

I

Woodeaton
Wood

Long
Wood

Sescut
Farm

Elsfiel

2

Home
Farm

Cherwell
Farm

3

28

Mill Lane

4

209

Cumberlege
Close

Park Way

Lodge Cl   Harlow
Wy

Church La   Butts La

Ponds
La

Little
Acreage

Marston

Elsfield   Road

Barns Hay

Cannons
Fld

PO

Southcroft

A40

B4150

5

ROAD

Oxford Road

Boults
La

Boults

53   54

E   F   34   G   H   NORTHERN BY-PASS ROAD

St Nicholas
Primary School

Rimmer
Close

Horseman Cl

Dents
Close

150 MARSH LANE

Oxford City
FC

OXSRAD

Stockleys
Rd

Dora Carr
Close

Matfield
Rd

Borrowmead
Rd

Sutton Rd

Northway
Health

John Buchan Rd

Westlands Drive

Foxwell
Dr

CHERWE

Elms
Drive

New Marston

Drive

gton
Drive

Rd

Blackwater Wood

E High Street

Beckley

F

G

H

New Inn Road

Sand Lane

Roman Wy

Woodperry

Beckley Court

Road

Bungalow Close

57

58

I

2

Woodperry

New Inn Farm

01

3

Stanton St John

B4027

Pound Lane

Mill Street

4

Cocks Lane

Middle Road

PO

Hillcraft Rd

Courtfield Road

PH

Shepherds Pit

PH

B4027

5

202

E

F

57

36

G Ashen Copse

58

H

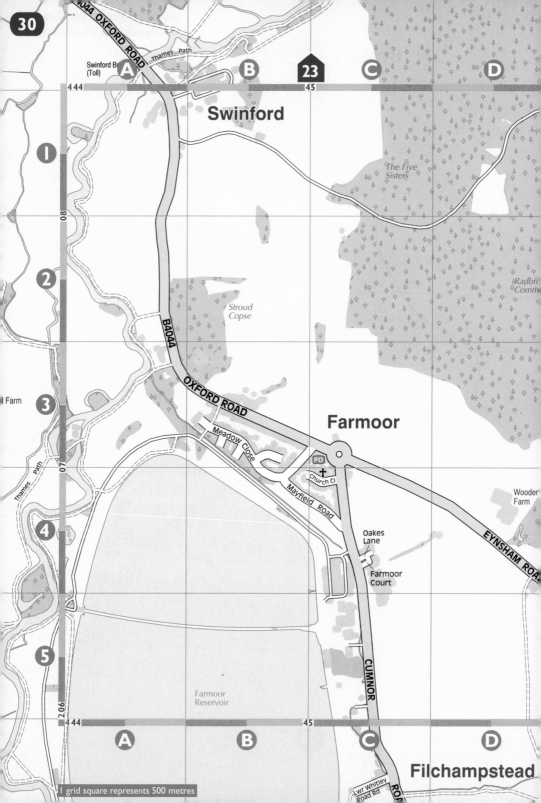

30

Swinford Br
(Toll)

A

Swinford

B

23

C

D

Thames Path

4 44

45

J44 OXFORD ROAD

08

1

The Five
Sisters

Radbro
Comm

2

B4044

Stroud
Copse

Farm

3

OXFORD ROAD

Farmoor

Thames Path

07

Meadow Close

PO

Church Cl

Wooder
Farm

Mayfield Road

Oakes
Lane

4

EYNSHAM ROA

Farmoor
Court

5

206

Farmoor
Reservoir

CUMNOR

4 44

45

A

B

C

D

Filchampstead

1 grid square represents 500 metres

Lwr Whitley
Road Rd

RO

32
Wytham

(A) (B) **25** Port Mead (C) (D)

4 48 49

Thames Path

River Thames or Isis

1

08

✝

Binsey

Thames Path

2

A34

WESTERN-BY-PASS-ROAD

Seacourt Stream

3

OX2

31

07

4

Tilbury Farm

Binsey Lane

A420

A420

Prestwich Pl

West Oxford Health Centre

Helen

5

Botley
Botley Medical Centre
Primary School

P+

Istake Cl

Industrial Estate

Trading Estate

Lamarsh Road

Earl St

Duke St

M Ct

Riverside Rd

Harley Rd

Oatlands Rd

Tilbury Lane

Hazel Rd

Poplar Road

Elms Road

Hinksey Business Centre

Lamarsh Rd

Works

Foxwell
Homestall
Hurdle Cl
Wortle Cl
Bushey Cl

Seacourt Road

WEST WAY

Church Way

Chd Wy

West Way Health Centre

PO

✝

Cemetery

39

New Botley

(C) (D)

4 48 49

B4044

Dean Court

Rose Gdns

(A)

SOUTHERN

(B)

Conifer Cl
Hurst
Spr

Arthray Road

Montagu Rd

Finmore Rd
St
Crs
Crabtr

Westminster

Varnell's Road

North Hinksey

Kings Mead Industrial Estate

I grid square represents 500 metres

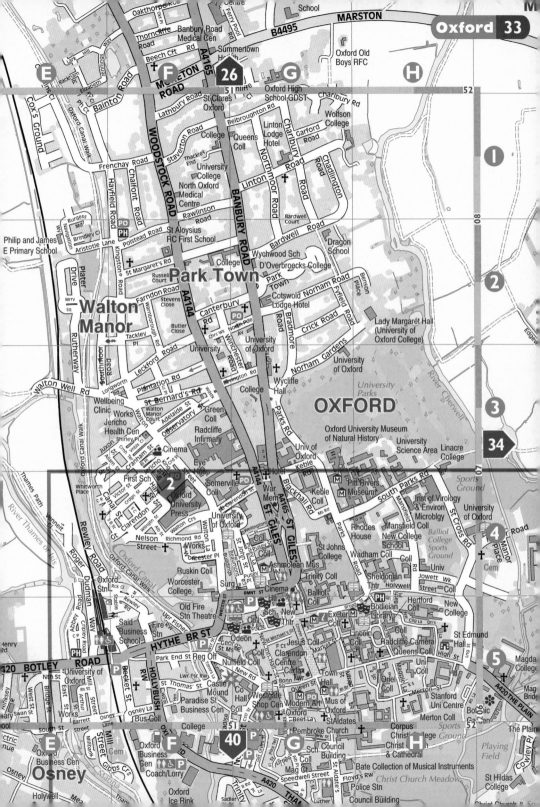

36

A B **29** C D
456 57

Oxford
Crematorium

1 Stowford

Ashen
Copse

Bayswater Road

d Rd
Mather Road
Bayswater Rd
Crane
Malford Road
Claymond Road
Routh Rd
Humfrey Rd
Watermill
Way
Bayswater
Farm Road

2
rton
Waynflete

Road
Gn
Ridges
Colwell
Dr
Burdell Av
Hill
View
Delbush Av
Merewood AV
Merewood AV
Elton
Cl

Sandhills

PO
Sandhills
Primary
School

Bayards Hill
Primary School
Ormerod
School
Hosker
Cl
Green
Ridges
Bush Cl
B CB

Merewood
AV

London Road

A40 LONDON ROAD

A40 LONDON ROAD

Downside End

P+

Thornhill Farm

London Road
Ridgeway Road
The
Link
The
Collinwood
Larches
Pathway
Downside Rd
Pond Cl
Ringwood Rd

Risinghurst

3

35
PO

Collinwood
Clo

Kiln

Grovelands
Rd

Shelley
Cl
Baker
Cl
Carter
Cl
Sermon
Cl
Richards
Way
Netherwoods Road
Lewis
Cl
Lane

4

Wychwood
La

otover
Kilns

5 Old Road

P
Shotover
Country Park

Shotover Plain

The
Ri

206

456 57

A B **43** C D

Old Road

1 grid square represents 500 metres

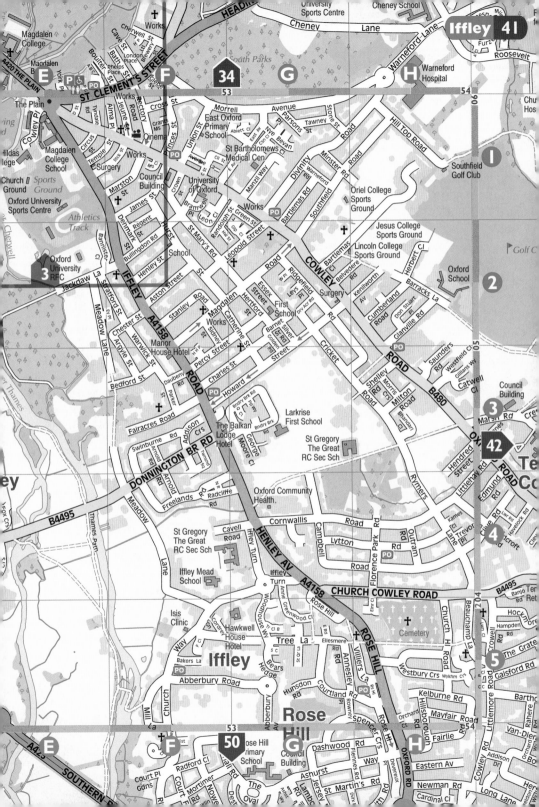

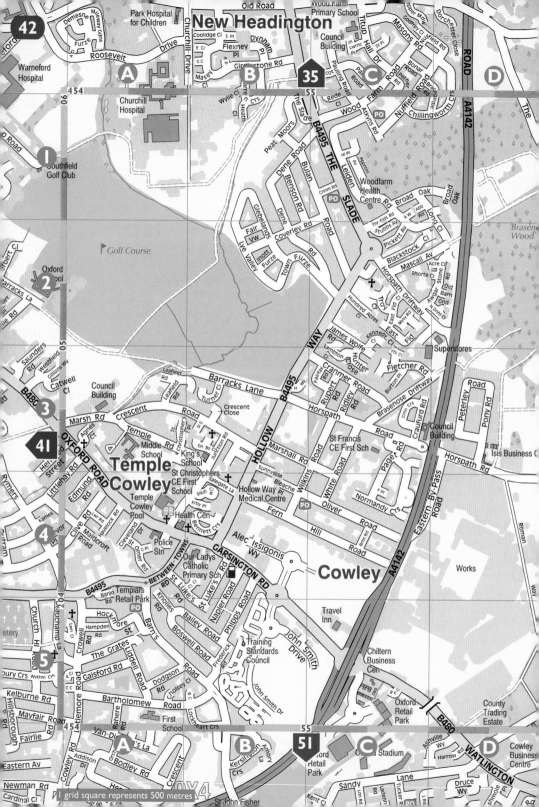

E
P
Dover Country Park
F
Shotover Plain
36
57
G
H
58
90

Old Road
I
Litt

Westhill Farm
Horspath Common
Blenheim Road
Blenheim
2
Gidley Wa

Open Basenose
Blenheim Wy
Spring La
Horspath CE Primary School
Butts Road
Collicutt Cl
05
Manor Farm Rd
Forde Cl
Wrightson Cl
Church Rd
PO
Manor Drive
Hill Rise
Centre Rd
Sunny Rd
Valley Rd
3

Horspath
Butler Close
44

Oxford Marathon RC
Horspath Athletics Track
Cuddesdon Rd
Cuddesdon

Road
4

204
5

E
F
57
52
G
H
58
City Farm

Northfield Farm
Oxford

Holton

E F G H

Wheatley
Business
Cen

Oxford Brookes University
(Wheatley Campus)

Holton
Mill

Old London Road

Anson Cl

Garden Centre

London Road

Cullum Rd

Ambrose Ri

Leyshon Rd

Miller Rd

The Av

Elm Cl

Myles La

Hillary Wy

Roman

Elton Crs

Road

A40

Wheatley
Bridge

Travelodge

Edon
Business

Oxford Servic

Sworford Lane

River Thame

River Thame

Cuddesdon Brook

E F G H

Eaton

Eaton
Heath

Surgery

Bablock Hythe Road

Eaton Road

444

45

Applet

A420

Appleton

**Bessels
Leigh**

Badswell
Lane

Town
Furlong Forge

Whites

Southby
Cl

Church
Rd

Eaton
Rd

PO

Appleton CE
Primary School

Manor
House

Park Lane

Horseshoes Cl

Fernplace
Close

Tubney
Manor Farm

Bessels Leigh
School

Row Leigh
Lane

I grid square represents 500 metres

48

A   B   39   C   D

4 48   49

Chilswell
Farm

Chilswell
House (Priory)

Chilswell Lane

1

Youlbury
Wood

2

3

47

Boars
Hill

Sandy Lane

Ridgeway

Bedwells
Heath

Jarn   Way

Berkeley Road

The Open
University

Hamels

Foxcombe
Hill

Orchard La

Brumcombe Lane

Wootton St ——s
CE Primary ——ol

4

5

Fox Lane

Lincombe Lane

Lincombe Lane

Sunningwell Road

Lamborough
Hill

A

Fox Lane

B

55

C

D

BOROUGH HILL

Sunningwell
School

Sunningwell

1 grid square represents 500 metres

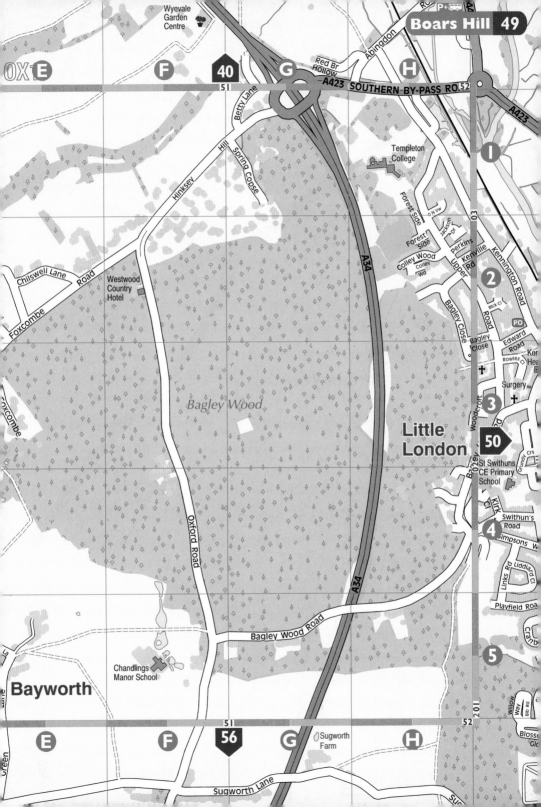

Wyevale Garden Centre

OXE E F **40** G
51

Red Br Hollow

Abingdon

H

A423 SOUTHERN-BY-PASS RO 52

A423

Betty Lane

Hinksey Hill

Spring Copse

A34

Templeton College

Forest Side

Jackson

N VW

Colley Wood
Colley Wd

Perkins

Kenville

Upper Rd

Kennington Road

I

Chilswell Lane

Road

Westwood Country Hotel

Foxcombe

Foxcombe

Bagley Wood

Bagley Close

Blick Cl

PO

Edward Road

Rowles

Ker Hea

Bagley Close

2

Surgery

Woodcroft

3

Little London

Bagley Rd

50

St Swithuns CE Primary School

Grundy Crs

Oxford Road

Bagley Wood Road

Kirk Cl

Swithun's Road

Simpsons La

4

Chandlings Manor School

Bayworth

Links Rd

Liddiard Cl

Playfield Roa

Cranb

5

Willow Way

Bib Rd

Blosse

Glo

51
E F **56** G H
52

Sugworth Farm

Sugworth Lane

201

Wheatley Road

Slay
Barn

E   F   **44**   G   H

59   60

City
Farm

Boundary
Business Park

Ripon
College

Church
Close

Cuddesdon

The Gn

I

2

Upperfield
Farm

High St

The Lane

PH

Wheatley Road

sington
Primary School

Garsington
Sports Club

Denton Lane

Denton Lane

Denton Hill

The Gn

Garsington

Denton

3

The Green

Southend

02

4

Southend

The Platt

5

201

Denton Lane

59   60

E   F   G   H

B480

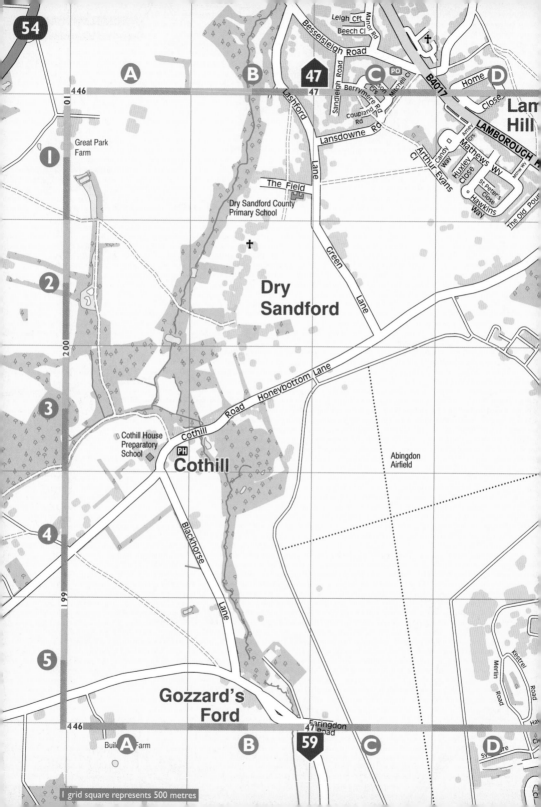

Lower Farm Lane

Lower Farm

Sandford Lane

The Avenue

Cranbrook Dr

The Paddock

The Av

William Way

more Crs

King Rd

Oak Av

Blossoms Gld

Fir Trees

Kennington Road

Thames Path

Park Farm

Chestnut Av

Kennington Road

The Copse

Radley CE Primary School

Church Road

Li Howe Cl

Turneys Cl

New Rd

shaws Copse

Ferry Close

St James Road

Selwyn Crs

Radley

Foxborough Road

Badgers Copse

Stonhous

Gooseacre

dale Close

Turners Close

Radley Station

Lower Radley

PO

Goose Acre Farm

Nuneham House

Thames Path

A   B   C   D

4 44   A338   45

Oakley Park

Golf Course

1

Frilford Heath

Frilford Heath
Golf Club

Sheepstead Folly

Sheepstead Farm

2

Sheepstead Road

Frilford

Joscas Preparatory School

3

Ford Lane

Kings Avenue   Longfields

The Farthings   North Way   Chaucer Wy   Duffield Pl   Howard   Cornish Road   Hyde copse

Marcham

Denman College

Fettiplace Rd   Haines Court   Orchard   Elwes Road   Morland Rd

New Rd   The Gap   Tower Cl   Marcham CE Primary School

4

FRILFORD ROAD

Cemetery

Church Street   All saints Cl   Park Side   sweet Briar   PO

A338

PACKHORSE LANE

Priory Lane

Mill Road

5

4 44   45

A   B   C   D

96   97   98

1 grid square represents 500 metres

E

Gozzard's Ford

F

54

G

H

Buildings Farm

Faringdon Road

47

Cholswell

Road

Hawthorne Av 48

Close

Sycamore

Faringdon Road

Chestnut Tree Close

Elm Tree Walk

Rookery Cl

I

Whitehouse Close

Cherry Tree

Shippon

2

Barrow Road

Sandford Brook

3

Blackla

Kimber

60

Fairacres

Way

P

Travel Inn

Abingdon Four Pillars Hotel

4

P

MARCHAM ROAD

A415

Abingdon Common

5

Meadow Farm House

River Ock

47

34

48

196

E

F

G

62

H

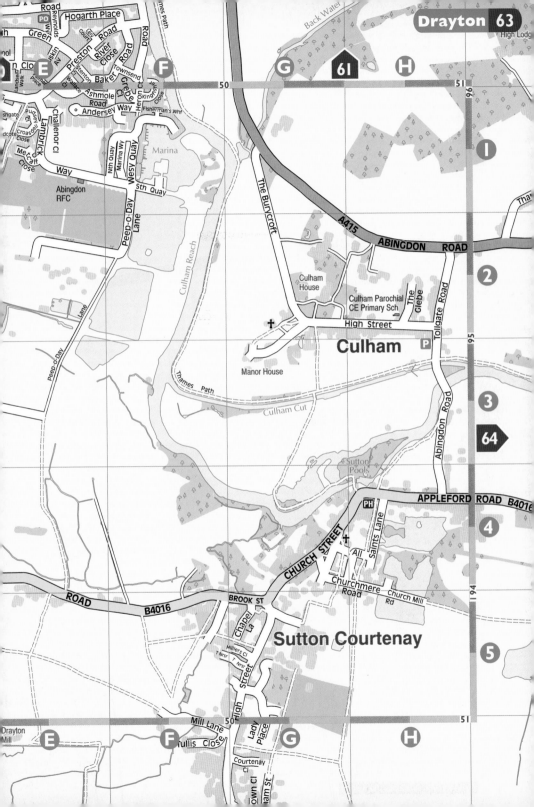

Thame Lane

E
F
G
H

54
55
96

The Culham Laboratory

Courtiers Green

Clifton Hampden

Watery Lane

PH

Surgery

I

Clifton Hampden CE Primary School

PO

Thames Path

High Street

2

Fullamoor

P

95

Clifton Lock

3

4

Little Wittenham Rd

Thames Path

Clifton Cut

Fieldside

94

Long Wittenham CE Primary School

Long Wittenham

5

High Street

Didcot Road

Fieldside

Pendon Museum

M
PO

Westfield Road

E
F
G
H

54
55

Sinodum Cl

Abingdon	60	B3	Cothill	54	A3	Grandpont	2	E7	New Hinksey	40	D3	Sunningwell	5
Abingdon Bridge	60	B4	Cowley	42	C4	Hampton Poyle	10	C2	Newland	21	F3	Sunnymead	2
Appleford	64	D5	Culham	63	G3	Harcourt Hill	39	G3	New Marston	34	A2	Sutton Courtenay	6
Appleton	46	A4	Cuddesdon	53	G1	Headington	35	E2	Northcourt	56	A5	Sutton Wick	6
Barton	35	H2	Cumnor Hill	39	E3	Hensington	5	E3	North Hinksey Village	39	G2	Swinford	2
Bayworth	49	E5	Cutteslowe	26	B1	Henwood	47	F3	North Leigh	12	B1	Temple Cowley	4
Begbroke	8	D4	Dean Court	38	D1	Horspath	43	H3	Old Woodstock	4	C2	Thrupp	
Bessels Leigh	46	D4	Denton	53	H3	Iffley	41	F5	Osney	40	A1	Upper Wolvercote	2
Binsey	32	C2	Drayton	62	B5	Islip	11	G4	Oxford	3	H3	Walton Manor	3
Blackbird Leys	51	F3	Dry Sandford	58	B2	Kennington	50	A3	Park Town	33	F2	Water Eaton	1
Bladon	8	A3	East End	6	D2	Kidlington	10	A4	The Platt	53	G5	Wheatley	4
Blenheim	43	G2	Eaton	46	B1	Lamborough Hill	54	D1	Radley	57	E5	Wildmoor	6
Blenheim	52	D2	Elsfield	28	A2	Little London	49	H3	Radley Park	56	C3	Witney	2
Boars Hill	48	A3	Eynsham	22	A3	Littlemore	51	E2	Risinghurst	36	A3	Wolvercote	2
Botley	32	A5	Farmoor	30	C3	Littleworth	44	A1	Rose Hill	41	G5	Woodeaton	1
Caldecott	60	C4	Forest Hill	37	F2	Long Hanborough	6	C4	Sandford-on-Thames	50	D5	Woodgreen	2
Campsfield	8	C3	Foxcombe Hill	48	C4	Long Wittenham	65	G5	Sandhills	36	B2	Woodstock	5
Cassington	23	F1	Freeland	13	C1	Lower Radley	57	G4	Shippon	59	H1	Wootton	4
Chawley	38	D5	Frilford Heath	58	B1	Marcham	58	C4	Southend	53	F4	Worton	1
Church Hanborough	14	B2	Garsington	53	E3	Marston	27	E5	South Hinksey	40	C4	Wytham	2
Clifton Hampden	65	G1	Gosford	17	H1	New Botley	39	G1	Stanton St John	29	G3	Yarnton	1
Cogges	21	G4	Gozzard's Ford	54	A5	New Headington	35	F5	Summertown	26	C5		

USING THE STREET INDEX

Street names are listed alphabetically. Each street name is followed by its postal town or area locality, the Postcode District, the page number, and the reference to the square in which the name is found.

Standard index entries are shown as follows:

Abberbury Av *COW/LTMR* OX4 ....**50** C1

Street names and selected addresses not shown on the map due to scale restrictions are shown in the index with an asterisk:

Arthur Garrard Cl *OXN/BOT/CM* OX2 * **33** F3

GENERAL ABBREVIATIONS

ACC	ACCESS	CUTT	CUTTINGS	HOL	HOLLOW	NW	NORTH WEST	SKWY	SKY
ALY	ALLEY	CV	COVE	HOSP	HOSPITAL	O/P	OVERPASS	SMT	SUM
AP	APPROACH	CVN	CANYON	HRB	HARBOUR	OFF	OFFICE	SOC	SOC
AR	ARCADE	DEPT	DEPARTMENT	HTH	HEATH	ORCH	ORCHARD	SP	S
ASS	ASSOCIATION	DL	DALE	HTS	HEIGHTS	OV	OVAL	SPR	SPR
AV	AVENUE	DM	DAM	HVN	HAVEN	PAL	PALACE	SQ	SQU
BCH	BEACH	DR	DRIVE	HWY	HIGHWAY	PAS	PASSAGE	ST	STF
BLDS	BUILDINGS	DRO	DROVE	IMP	IMPERIAL	PAV	PAVILION	STN	STAT
BND	BEND	DRY	DRIVEWAY	IN	INLET	PDE	PARADE	STR	STRE
BNK	BANK	DWGS	DWELLINGS	IND EST	INDUSTRIAL ESTATE	PH	PUBLIC HOUSE	STRD	STRD
BR	BRIDGE	E	EAST	INF	INFIRMARY	PK	PARK	SW	SOUTH W
BRK	BROOK	EMB	EMBANKMENT	INFO	INFORMATION	PKWY	PARKWAY	TDG	TRAD
BTM	BOTTOM	EMBY	EMBASSY	INT	INTERCHANGE	PL	PLACE	TER	TERR
BUS	BUSINESS	ESP	ESPLANADE	IS	ISLAND	PLN	PLAIN	THWY	THROUGH
BVD	BOULEVARD	EST	ESTATE	JCT	JUNCTION	PLNS	PLAINS	TNL	TUN
BY	BYPASS	EX	EXCHANGE	JTY	JETTY	PLZ	PLAZA	TOLL	TOLL
CATH	CATHEDRAL	EXPY	EXPRESSWAY	KG	KING	POL	POLICE STATION	TPK	TURNF
CEM	CEMETERY	EXT	EXTENSION	KNL	KNOLL	PREC	PRECINCT	TR	TR
CEN	CENTRE	F/O	FLYOVER	LA	LANE	PREP	PREPARATORY	TRL	TRL
CFT	CROFT	FC	FOOTBALL CLUB	LDG	LODGE	PRIM	PRIMARY	TWR	TWR
CH	CHURCH	FK	FORK	LGT	LIGHT	PROM	PROMENADE	U/P	UNDERF
CHA	CHASE	FLD	FIELD	LK	LOCK	PRS	PRINCESS	UNI	UNIVERS
CHYD	CHURCHYARD	FLDS	FIELDS	LKS	LAKES	PRT	PORT	UPR	UP
CIR	CIRCLE	FLS	FALLS	LNDG	LANDING	PT	POINT	V	V
CIRC	CIRCUS	FLS	FLATS	LTL	LITTLE	PTH	PATH	VA	VAL
CL	CLOSE	FM	FARM	LWR	LOWER	PZ	PIAZZA	VIAD	VIAD
CLFS	CLIFFS	FT	FORT	MAG	MAGISTRATE	QD	QUADRANT	VIL	VI
CMP	CAMP	FWY	FREEWAY	MAN	MANSIONS	QU	QUEEN	VIS	VI
CNR	CORNER	FY	FERRY	MD	MEAD	QY	QUAY	VLG	VILL
CO	COUNTY	GA	GATE	MDW	MEADOWS	R	RIVER	VW	VIE
COLL	COLLEGE	GAL	GALLERY	MEM	MEMORIAL	RBT	ROUNDABOUT	W	W
COM	COMMON	GDN	GARDEN	MKT	MARKET	RD	ROAD	WD	WC
COMM	COMMISSION	GDNS	GARDENS	MKTS	MARKETS	RDG	RIDGE	WHF	WHA
CON	CONVENT	GLD	GLADE	ML	MALL	REP	REPUBLIC	WK	WK
COT	COTTAGE	GLN	GLEN	ML	MILL	RES	RESERVOIR	WKS	WA
COTS	COTTAGES	GN	GREEN	MNR	MANOR	RFC	RUGBY FOOTBALL CLUB	WLS	WLS
CP	CAPE	GND	GROUND	MS	MEWS	RI	RISE	WY	V
CPS	COPSE	GRA	GRANGE	MSN	MISSION	RP	RAMP	YD	YA
CR	CREEK	GRG	GARAGE	MT	MOUNT	RW	ROW	YHA	YOUTH HOS
CREM	CREMATORIUM	GT	GREAT	MTN	MOUNTAIN	S	SOUTH		
CRS	CRESCENT	GTWY	GATEWAY	MTS	MOUNTAINS	SCH	SCHOOL		
CSWY	CAUSEWAY	GV	GROVE	MUS	MUSEUM	SE	SOUTH EAST		
CT	COURT	HGR	HIGHER	MWY	MOTORWAY	SER	SERVICE AREA		
CTRL	CENTRAL	HL	HILL	N	NORTH	SH	SHORE		
CTS	COURTS	HLS	HILLS	NE	NORTH EAST	SHOP	SHOPPING		
CTYD	COURTYARD	HO	HOUSE						

POSTCODE TOWNS AND AREA ABBREVIATIONS

ABGD	Abingdon	KID	Kidlington	OX/KTN	Oxford/Kennington	RW/EYN	Rural Witney/Eynsham	WHLY	Whea
COW/LTMR	Cowley/Littlemore	MCHM/KBPZ	Marcham/Kingston Bagpuize	OXN/BOT/CM	Oxford north/Botley/Cumnor	STAD	Stadhampton	WITNEY	Wit
HEAD	Headington					WDSTK	Woodstock		

A

erbury Av COW/LTMR OX4 .....50 C1
erbury Rd COW/LTMR OX4 ....41 F5
ey Cl OX14 ....60 D3
ey Cl OX14 ....60 D3
RW/EYN OX29 ....22 C4
ey Rd OXN/BOT/CM OX2 ......20 A3
WITNEY OX28 ....20 C3
ey St RW/EYN OX29 ....22 C4
ots Wood (East)
 ....42 C1
ots Wood (West)
 ....42 C1
ort Rd ABGD OX14 ....60 D2
hwood Rd RW/EYN OX29 ....6 A4
ngdon Br ABGD OX14 ....9 H4
ngdon Rd ABGD OX14 ....40 D3
OX/KTN OX1 ....40 D3
on Cl ABGD OX14 ....38 A4
ert Cl COW/LTMR OX4 ....35 E5
and Cl HEAD OX3 ....35 E5
e Cl HEAD OX3 ....42 C2
e End St RW/EYN OX29 ....22 B4
emead Rd WHLY OX33 ....44 A1
llison Crs COW/LTMR OX4 .....41 F5
llison Dr COW/LTMR OX4 ....51 E1
aidale St OXN/BOT/CM OX2 ..33 F3
nes Ct COW/LTMR OX4 ....42 A3
n Bullock Cl HEAD OX3 ....3 J4
ert St OXN/BOT/CM OX2 ....2 B1
ert St HEAD OX3 ....35 H2
barton Dr HEAD OX3 ....35 H2
en Crs HEAD OX3 ....35 H2
rich Rd OXN/BOT/CM OX2 .....26 D5
sworth Ct WITNEY OX28 ....20 C3
c Issigonis Wy
 COW/LTMR OX4 ....42 B4
sworth Gv HEAD OX3 ....34 D1
xander Cl ABGD OX14 ....56 A4
xandra Rd OXN/BOT/CM OX2 .32 D5
red St OX/KTN OX1 ....1 G5
e Smith Sq COW/LTMR OX4 ..51 E2
am St OXN/BOT/CM OX2 ....33 E3
der Cl ABGD OX14 ....55 E5
dromeda Cl COW/LTMR OX4 ..51 H3
emone Cl COW/LTMR OX4 ......51 H4
gelica Cl COW/LTMR OX4 ....51 H4
na Pavlova Cl ABGD OX14 ......60 B3
he Greenwood Cl
 COW/LTMR OX4 ....41 G4
nesley Rd COW/LTMR OX4 .....51 H3
son Cl MCHM/KBPZ OX13 .....58 D4
WHLY OX33 ....45 E5
ce Wy WITNEY OX28 ....20 C5
pleford Dr ABGD OX14 ....56 B5
pleford Rd HEAD OX3 ....63 H4
pletree Cl COW/LTMR OX4 ....51 H4
sley Rd COW/LTMR OX4 ....42 B4
gentan Cl ABGD OX14 ....62 D1
ngyle St COW/LTMR OX4 ....41 F2
stute La OXN/BOT/CM OX2 ....33 F3
ington Dr HEAD OX3 ....34 A1
mstrong Rd COW/LTMR OX4 .50 D3
nold Rd COW/LTMR OX4 ....41 F5
nold's Wy OXN/BOT/CM OX2 .26 C5
hray Rd OXN/BOT/CM OX2 .....39 E1
hur Evans Cl
 MCHM/KBPZ OX13 ....54 C1
hur Garrard Cl
 OXN/BOT/CM OX2 * 33 F3
hur St COW/LTMR OX4 ....2 A4
n Cl KID OX5 ....17 G1
hcombe Cl WITNEY OX28 ....21 H5
ncroft Cl OXN/BOT/CM OX2 ...31 H5
henden Cl ABGD OX14 ....61 G1
ngate ABGD OX14 ....63 E1
n Gv HEAD OX3 ....35 F2
hlong Rd HEAD OX3 ....34 C1
hmole PI COW/LTMR OX4 ......51 H3
hmole Rd ABGD OX14 ....63 E1
hurst Wy COW/LTMR OX4 .....50 C1
oen Sq COW/LTMR OX4 ....51 G1
quith Rd COW/LTMR OX4 ....51 G4
tley Av KID OX5 ....17 H2
bin Cl ABGD OX14 ....60 D3
ston Cl COW/LTMR OX4 ....41 F2
kinson Cl HEAD OX3 ....35 G1
kyns Rd HEAD OX3 ....42 C1
well PI HEAD OX3 ....35 F5
diett Dr ABGD OX14 ....55 G5
venue Four WITNEY OX28 ......21 F4
venue One WITNEY OX28 ....21 E5
e Avenue OX/KTN OX1 ....30 A5
WHLY OX33 ....45 E2
venue Three WITNEY OX28 ....21 F4
venue Two WITNEY OX28 ....21 E5
or Rd MCHM/KBPZ OX13 ....55 E4
vgar Stone Rd HEAD OX3 ....42 C2
tell Cl KID OX5 ....9 H4
alea Av KID OX5 ....16 D2

B

Back La RW/EYN OX29 ....22 C4
Badger Cl WHLY OX33 ....37 E2
Badgers Copse ABGD OX14 .....57 E5
Badswell La MCHM/KBPZ OX13 .46 A4
Bagley Cl OX/KTN OX1 ....49 H5
Bagley Wood Rd OX/KTN OX1 .49 G5
Bailey Rd COW/LTMR OX4 ....42 A4
Baillie Cl ABGD OX14 ....60 C4
Bainton Rd OXN/BOT/CM OX2 .33 E1
Baker Cl HEAD OX3 ....35 H4
Baker Rd ABGD OX14 ....60 C5
Bakers La COW/LTMR OX4 ....41 F5
Bakers Piece WITNEY OX28 .....21 F1
Balfour Rd COW/LTMR OX4 .....51 G1
Ballard Cha ABGD OX14 ....56 A4
Ballic Whf OX/KTN OX1 ....2 D6
Bampton Cl ABGD OX14 ....51 E1
Banbury Ct ABGD OX14 ....60 D3
Banbury Rd KID OX5 ....9 H4
 OXN/BOT/CM OX2 ....33 F1
 WDSTK OX20 ....5 E4
Banjo Rd COW/LTMR OX4 ....42 A4
Bankside HEAD OX3 ....35 G3
 RW/EYN OX29 ....9 F4
Bannister Cl COW/LTMR OX4 ...22 C4
Bardwell Ct OXN/BOT/CM OX2 .33 G1
Bardwell Rd OXN/BOT/CM OX2 .33 G1
Barfleur Cl ABGD OX14 ....56 B4
Barleycott La COW/LTMR OX4 .40 C5
Barlow Cl WHLY OX33 ....44 B1
Barn Cl KID OX5 ....9 H5
 OXN/BOT/CM OX2 ....38 D3
Barnet St COW/LTMR OX4 ....41 G2
Barns Hay HEAD OX3 ....27 F5
Barn's Rd COW/LTMR OX4 ....42 A5
Barracks La COW/LTMR OX4 ....41 H2
 COW/LTMR OX4 ....42 B3
Barrett St OXN/BOT/CM OX2 ...33 H1
Barrington Cl HEAD OX3 ....35 E4
 WITNEY OX28 ....20 C4
Barrow Hill Cl ABGD OX14 ......54 C5
Barrow Rd MCHM/KBPZ OX13 .59 G2
Bartholomew Av KID OX5 ....16 C5
Bartholomew Rd RW/EYN OX29 .22 B3
Bartholomew Rd
 ABGD OX14 ....42 A5
Bartlemas Cl COW/LTMR OX4 ..41 G2
Bartlemas Rd COW/LTMR OX4 .41 G2
Bartlett Cl WITNEY OX28 ....20 C5
Barton La ABGD OX14 ....61 G3
Barton Rd HEAD OX3 ....35 G2
Barton Village Rd HEAD OX3 ....35 F1
Bassett Rd HEAD OX3 ....35 G3
Basset Wy KID OX5 ....10 B4
Bateman St HEAD OX3 ....35 E4
Bath Ct ABGD OX14 ....60 C3
Bath PI OX/KTN OX1 ....3 G3
Bath St COW/LTMR OX4 ....60 D3
Bayswater Farm Rd HEAD OX3 .36 A2
Bayswater Rd HEAD OX3 ....35 H2
Beagle Cl ABGD OX14 ....46 C5
Beagles Cl KID OX5 ....18 A1
Bear Cl WDSTK OX20 ....4 D4
Bear La OX/KTN OX1 ....2 E4
Bears Hedge COW/LTMR OX4 ...41 H5
Beauchamp La COW/LTMR OX4 .41 H5
Beaumont Buildings
 OX/KTN OX1 ....2 C1
Beaumont La OX/KTN OX1 ....2 D2
Beaumont PI OX/KTN OX1 * 2 D2
Beaumont Rd HEAD OX3 ....35 G5
Beaumont St OX/KTN OX1 ....2 C2
Becket St OX/KTN OX1 ....2 A1
Becketts Cl RW/EYN OX29 ....6 B4
Beckley Ct ABGD OX14 ....29 F1
Bedford St COW/LTMR OX4 .....41 F2
Bedwells Heath OX/KTN OX1 ....48 B3
Beech Cl ABGD OX14 ....55 H5
Beech Crs KID OX5 ....17 G2
Beech Croft Rd
 OXN/BOT/CM OX2 ....26 B5
The Beeches HEAD OX3 ....35 G2
Beech Rd WITNEY OX28 ....21 E3
Beechgate WITNEY OX28 ....21 E5
Beeching Wy WHLY OX33 * 44 C1
Beech Rd HEAD OX3 ....35 G2
 OXN/BOT/CM OX2 ....39 F2
 RW/EYN OX29 ....22 C3
 WHLY OX33 ....44 D2
 WITNEY OX28 ....20 D3
Beef La OX/KTN OX1 ....2 D3
Beggarbush Crs KID OX5 ....9 F4
Belbroughton Rd
 OXN/BOT/CM OX2 ....33 F1
Belgrove Cl KID OX5 ....9 G5
Bell Cl RW/EYN OX29 ....23 H1
Bellenger Wy KID OX5 ....23 H1
Bell La OX/KTN OX1 ....44 D1
 WHLY OX33 ....44 D1
Belvedere Rd COW/LTMR OX4 .41 G2
Ben Cl KID OX5 ....9 G5
Benmead Rd KID OX5 ....10 A4
Bennett Crs COW/LTMR OX4 ....42 B4
Benson Pl OXN/BOT/CM OX2 ...33 G1
Benson Rd ABGD OX14 ....55 G5
 HEAD OX3 ....42 B1
Bergamont Pl COW/LTMR OX4 .42 A4
Bergen Av ABGD OX14 ....62 D1
Berkeley Rd OX/KTN OX1 ....48 C5
Bernard Cl KID OX5 ....17 E5
Bernwood Rd HEAD OX3 ....35 G2
Berry Cl OXN/BOT/CM OX2 ......51 H1
Berry Cft ABGD OX14 ....60 C1
Berrymere Rd
 MCHM/KBPZ OX13 ....47 G5
Bertie Pl OXN/BOT/CM OX2 .....40 D4
Bertie Rd OXN/BOT/CM OX2 ....38 B4

Besselsleigh Rd
 MCHM/KBPZ OX13 ....47 E4
Betty La OX/KTN OX1 ....49 G1
Between Towns Rd
 COW/LTMR OX4 ....42 A4
Beverley Cl ABGD OX14 ....60 C1
Bevington Rd
 OXN/BOT/CM OX2 ....33 F3
Bhandari Cl COW/LTMR OX4 ....41 H5
Bibury Cl WITNEY OX28 ....20 B3
Bicester Rd KID OX5 ....17 H1
Bickerton Rd HEAD OX3 ....35 E4
Big Wood Pk ABGD OX14 * 57 E1
Binsey La OXN/BOT/CM OX2 ...32 C4
Binswood Av HEAD OX3 ....35 G4
Birchfield Cl COW/LTMR OX4 ...41 H5
Birch Rd STAD OX44 ....52 D2
Birdlip Cl WITNEY OX28 ....20 B2
Biscoe Ct WHLY OX33 ....45 E1
Bishop Kirk Pl
 OXN/BOT/CM OX2 ....26 A4
Bittern Wy RW/EYN OX29 ....29 G1
Blackberry La STAD OX44 ....52 A4
Blackbird Leys Rd
 COW/LTMR OX4 ....51 G2
Blackfriars Rd OX/KTN OX1 ....2 D6
Blackhall Rd OX/KTN OX1 ....2 D1
Blackhorse La
 MCHM/KBPZ OX13 ....54 A4
Blacklands Wy ABGD OX14 ....60 A3
Blackman Cl OX/KTN OX1 ....50 A2
Blacknall Rd ABGD OX14 ....60 B3
Blacksmiths Meadow
 ....51 H3
Blackstock Cl HEAD OX3 ....42 C2
Blackthorn Cl HEAD OX3 ....35 F2
Bladon Cl OXN/BOT/CM OX2 ...25 H5
Bladon Rd WDSTK OX20 ....8 B1
Blakes Av WITNEY OX28 ....21 H4
Blandford Av OXN/BOT/CM OX2 .26 A2
Blandford Rd KID OX5 ....9 H5
Blankstone Cl RW/EYN OX29 ...22 B4
Blay Cl COW/LTMR OX4 ....51 G1
Bleache Pl COW/LTMR OX4 ......42 B4
Blenheim Dr OXN/BOT/CM OX2 .26 A3
 WITNEY OX28 ....20 C4
Blenheim La RW/EYN OX29 .....13 G2
Blenheim Rd KID OX5 ....10 B5
 WHLY OX33 ....43 G2
Blenheim Wy OX/KTN OX1 ....2 D2
Bletchingdon Rd KID OX5 ....10 C1
 KID OX5 ....11 G2
Blomfield Pl OXN/BOT/CM OX2 .33 F3
Blossoms Gld ABGD OX14 ....57 E1
The Blowings RW/EYN OX29 ....13 G1
Bluebell Ct COW/LTMR OX4 .....51 H5
Bluebell Ride ABGD OX14 ....60 A5
Blue Boar St OX/KTN OX1 ....2 D4
Bobby Fryer Cl COW/LTMR OX4 .42 C5
Bodley Rd COW/LTMR OX4 ....51 E1
Bolsover Cl RW/EYN OX29 ....6 A4
Bolton's La RW/EYN OX29 ....6 C2
Bonar Rd HEAD OX3 ....35 G5
Bonn Sq OX/KTN OX1 ....2 D4
Book End RW/EYN OX29 ....20 A2
Boreford Rd ABGD OX14 ....56 B5
Borough Wk ABGD OX14 ....60 A5
Borrowmead Rd HEAD OX3 ....34 D1
Bostock Rd ABGD OX14 ....60 B3
Boswell Rd COW/LTMR OX4 .....42 A5
Botley Rd OXN/BOT/CM OX2 ......2 A4
Bottom Rd RW/EYN OX29 ....22 B5
The Boulevard KID OX5 ....9 F3
Boulter Dr ABGD OX14 ....56 A4
Boulter St COW/LTMR OX4 ....3 J4
Boults La HEAD OX3 ....34 B1
Boults Rd HEAD OX3 ....34 B1
Boundary Brook Rd
 COW/LTMR OX4 ....41 G3
Boundary Cl WDSTK OX20 ....4 D4
Bourlon Wd ABGD OX14 ....60 B1
Bourne Cl OXN/BOT/CM OX2 ...26 B2
Bourton Cl WITNEY OX28 ....20 C5
Bowerman Cl KID OX5 ....9 H5
Bowgrave Copse ABGD OX14 ...61 G1
Bowness Av HEAD OX3 ....34 D2
Bowyer Rd ABGD OX14 ....60 D2
Boxhill Rd ABGD OX14 ....60 C2
Boxhill Wk ABGD OX14 ....60 C2
Boxwell Cl ABGD OX14 ....60 A5
Bracegirdle Rd HEAD OX3 ....35 G5
Bradmore Rd OXN/BOT/CM OX2 .33 G2
Brake Hl COW/LTMR OX4 ....52 A3
Bramble Bank RW/EYN OX29 ....21 H1
Brambling Wy COW/LTMR OX4 .51 H5
Bramley Hts WITNEY OX28 * 20 D5
Brampton Cl ABGD OX14 ....60 C1
Brampton Rd ABGD OX14 ....35 G2
Bramwell Pl COW/LTMR OX4 ....41 F1
Brandon Cl KID OX5 ....9 H5
Brasenose Driftway
 COW/LTMR OX4 ....42 C3
Brasenose Dr KID OX5 ....10 B4
Brasenose La OX/KTN OX1 * 2 D3
Brewers Ct ABGD OX14 ....60 C3
Brewer St OX/KTN OX1 ....2 D4
Briar Cl KID OX5 ....9 G5
Briar End KID OX5 ....9 G5
Briar Thicket WDSTK OX20 ....5 E4
Briar Wy COW/LTMR OX4 ....51 H2
Bridewell Cl RW/EYN OX29 ....12 A1
Bridges Cl ABGD OX14 ....60 A5
Bridge St ABGD OX14 ....60 D4
 KID OX5 ....17 G1
 OXN/BOT/CM OX2 ....33 E5
 RW/EYN OX29 ....22 F2
Brindley Cl OXN/BOT/CM OX2 ..33 E2
Broad Cl KID OX5 ....31 H5
 OXN/BOT/CM OX2 ....26 B3
Broad Field Rd KID OX5 ....16 D2
Broadfields COW/LTMR OX4 .....35 E4
Broadmead Pl HEAD OX3 ....34 D1
Broadhurst Gdns
 COW/LTMR OX4 ....50 C3

Broad Marsh La RW/EYN OX29 .13 G2
Broad Oak HEAD OX3 ....42 D1
Broad St ABGD OX14 ....60 D3
 OX/KTN OX1 ....2 D3
The Broadway KID OX5 ....17 H3
Broadway Cl WITNEY OX28 ......20 D2
Brocklesby Rd COW/LTMR OX4 .50 C2
Brode Cl ABGD OX14 ....56 B5
Brogden Cl OXN/BOT/CM OX2 .33 G2
Brome Pl HEAD OX3 ....35 G2
Brookfield Crs HEAD OX3 ....34 C1
Brook Hl WDSTK OX20 ....4 D4
Brooklime Wk COW/LTMR OX4 .51 H5
Brookside ABGD OX14 ....60 D1
 HEAD OX3 ....35 E4
Brook St ABGD OX14 ....63 G5
 OX/KTN OX1 ....2 F7
Brook Vw COW/LTMR OX4 ....52 A2
Brook Wy RW/EYN OX29 ....21 H1
Broughtons Cl HEAD OX3 ....34 B1
Browns Cl OXN/BOT/CM OX2 ...38 C2
Brown's La WITNEY OX28 ....21 E2
Brumcombe La OX/KTN OX1 .....48 D3
Bryony Cl COW/LTMR OX4 ....52 A2
Buckingham St OX/KTN OX1 ....2 D5
Buckland Ms ABGD OX14 ....60 B3
Buckler Pl COW/LTMR OX4 ....55 G2
Buckler Rd OXN/BOT/CM OX2 ..26 B3
Bucklers Bury Rd ABGD OX14 ...56 B5
Buckles Cl ABGD OX14 ....60 A2
Budds Cl WDSTK OX20 ....5 E5
Bulan Rd HEAD OX3 ....42 B1
Bullingdon Rd COW/LTMR OX4 .41 G2
Bullsmead MCHM/KBPZ OX13 ..55 G2
Bullstake Cl OXN/BOT/CM OX2 .32 D5
Bulrush Rd COW/LTMR OX4 ......51 H2
Bulwarks La OX/KTN OX1 ....2 C3
Bungalow Cl HEAD OX3 ....29 G1
Burbush Rd COW/LTMR OX4 .....51 H2
Burchester Av HEAD OX3 ....35 G2
Burdell Av HEAD OX3 ....36 A3
Burford Rd WITNEY OX28 ....20 A2
Burgan Cl COW/LTMR OX4 ....42 B5
Burgess Md OXN/BOT/CM OX2 .36 A3
Burlington Crs HEAD OX3 ....36 A3
Burra Cl COW/LTMR OX4 ....50 C5
Burrows Cl HEAD OX3 ....35 F5
Bursill Cl HEAD OX3 ....36 A2
Burton Cl ABGD OX14 ....60 A4
Burton Pl COW/LTMR OX4 ....42 C3
Burwell Cl WITNEY OX28 ....20 C4
Burwell Dr WITNEY OX28 ....20 C4
Burwell Meadow WITNEY OX28 .20 C5
The Burycroft ABGD OX14 ....63 G1
Bury St ABGD OX14 ....60 A5
Busby Cl RW/EYN OX29 ....9 H1
Buscot Dr ABGD OX14 ....56 A5
Bushey Cl OXN/BOT/CM OX2 ...31 H5
Bushey Leys Cl HEAD OX3 ....35 G1
Butler Cl OXN/BOT/CM OX2 .....38 A3
 WHLY OX33 ....43 H3
Buttercup Sq COW/LTMR OX4 ..51 H5
Butterwort Pl COW/LTMR OX4 ..51 H2
Butterwyke Pl OX/KTN OX1 * 2 E5
Butts La HEAD OX3 ....27 F5
Butts Rd WHLY OX33 ....43 G3
Byron Cl ABGD OX14 ....60 D1

C

Cadogan Pk WDSTK OX20 ....4 C3
Calcot Cl HEAD OX3 ....35 G5
Caldecott Cl ABGD OX14 ....60 B4
Caldecott Ct ABGD OX14 ....60 C4
Caldecott Rd ABGD OX14 ....60 C4
Calves Cl KID OX5 ....9 H5
Cambridge Ter OX/KTN OX1 * 2 E4
Cameron Av ABGD OX14 ....61 G1
Campbell Rd COW/LTMR OX4 ...41 G4
Campbells Cl WDSTK OX20 ....5 E4
Campden Cl WITNEY OX28 ....20 C2
Campion Rd ABGD OX14 ....60 D2
Campion Wy RW/EYN OX29 .....21 H1
Canal Rd KID OX5 ....9 F1
Canal St OXN/BOT/CM OX2 ......33 F3
Candy Wy MCHM/KBPZ OX13 ..54 D1
Canning Crs OX/KTN OX1 ....41 E4
Cannons Fld HEAD OX3 ....27 F5
Canterbury Rd
 OXN/BOT/CM OX2 ....33 F2
Capel Cl OXN/BOT/CM OX2 .....26 A3
Cardigan St OXN/BOT/CM OX2 ..2 B1
Cardinal Cl COW/LTMR OX4 .....50 D2
Cardwell Crs HEAD OX3 ....35 G4
Carey Cl OXN/BOT/CM OX2 .....25 H2
Carillon Rd OXN/BOT/CM OX2 ..26 B2
Carline St OX/KTN OX1 ....2 E4
Caroline St COW/LTMR OX4 ....3 J4
Carpenter Cl COW/LTMR OX4 ...51 G2
Carse Cl ABGD OX14 ....56 B4
Carter Cl HEAD OX3 ....35 G2
Cassington Rd KID OX5 ....16 C4
 RW/EYN OX29 ....9 F5
Castle St OX/KTN OX1 ....2 C4
Catherine Cl ABGD OX14 ....57 F4
Catherine St COW/LTMR OX4 ....41 F2
Catte St OX/KTN OX1 ....2 E3
Catwell Cl OXN/BOT/CM OX2 ...29 H5
Caudwell Cl ABGD OX14 ....62 B4
The Causeway WDSTK OX20 ....4 C3
Cave St COW/LTMR OX4 ....3 K4
Cecil Sharpe Cl HEAD OX3 ....35 E4
Cedar Dr RW/EYN OX29 ....21 H1
Cedar Rd ABGD OX14 ....39 E2
Celandine Pl COW/LTMR OX4 ...51 H3

Cemetery Rd ABGD OX14 ....60 B3
Centaury Pl COW/LTMR OX4 ....52 A2
Centre Ri WHLY OX33 ....43 H5
Chadlington Rd
 OXN/BOT/CM OX2 ....33 G1
Chaffinch Wk COW/LTMR OX4 * .51 H3
Chain Aly OX/KTN OX1 * 2 D3
Chalfont Rd OXN/BOT/CM OX2 .33 F1
Challenor Cl ABGD OX14 ....63 E1
Chamberlain Pl KID OX5 ....9 G4
Champion Cl COW/LTMR OX4 ...51 H3
Champion Wy COW/LTMR OX4 .50 D2
Champs Cl ABGD OX14 ....56 C5
Chancel Wy MCHM/KBPZ OX13 .58 C5
Chandlers Cl ABGD OX14 ....61 G1
Chapel La ABGD OX14 ....60 B4
 COW/LTMR OX4 ....50 C2
Chapel St COW/LTMR OX4 ....41 F1
Chapel Wy OXN/BOT/CM OX2 ..32 B5
Charlbury Cl KID OX5 ....9 H3
Charlbury Rd OXN/BOT/CM OX2 .33 G1
Charles St COW/LTMR OX4 ....41 G2
Charney Av ABGD OX14 ....56 B5
The Charter ABGD OX14 ....60 D3
Chatham Rd OX/KTN OX1 ....40 D4
Chaunterell Wy ABGD OX14 ......60 A4
Chawley La OXN/BOT/CM OX2 ..38 B3
Checker Wk ABGD OX14 * 60 D3
Chedworth Dr WITNEY OX28 ....20 C2
Cheers Farm ABGD OX14 ....62 C4
Cheney La HEAD OX3 ....34 C5
Chequers Pl HEAD OX3 ....35 G3
Cherry Cl ABGD OX14 ....51 H5
 KID OX5 ....17 G1
Cherry Tree Dr
 MCHM/KBPZ OX13 ....60 A1
Cherwell Av KID OX5 ....10 C5
Cherwell Cl ABGD OX14 ....61 F1
Cherwell Dr HEAD OX3 ....34 B1
Cherwell St HEAD OX3 ....3 K3
Chester St COW/LTMR OX4 ....41 F2
Chestnut Av ABGD OX14 ....57 E5
 HEAD OX3 ....35 F2
Chestnut Cl WITNEY OX28 ....21 F1
Chestnut Rd OXN/BOT/CM OX2 .39 F2
The Chestnuts ABGD OX14 ....61 G1
Cheyney Wk ABGD OX14 ....60 A1
Chiers Dr ABGD OX14 ....62 C4
Chilbridge Rd RW/EYN OX29 ....22 A4
Childrey Wy ABGD OX14 ....56 B5
Chillingworth Crs HEAD OX3 .....42 C1
Chilswell La OX/KTN OX1 ....48 D1
Chilswell Rd COW/LTMR OX4 ....40 C2
Chilton Cl ABGD OX14 ....61 F1
Cholesbury Gra HEAD OX3 ....34 C2
Cholsey Cl COW/LTMR OX4 ......42 A5
Cholswell Rd MCHM/KBPZ OX13 .55 E5
Chorefields KID OX5 ....9 H4
Choswell Spring
 COW/LTMR OX4 * 51 G3
Church Cl KID OX5 ....11 G5
 OX/KTN OX1 ....30 B4
 STAD OX44 ....53 H1
Church Cowley Rd
 COW/LTMR OX4 ....41 G4
Church Hill Rd COW/LTMR OX4 .41 H5
Churchill Cl WDSTK OX20 ....4 D3
Churchill Dr HEAD OX3 ....35 E5
Churchill Ga WDSTK OX20 ....5 E4
Churchill Pl OXN/BOT/CM OX2 ..25 H5
Churchill Rd KID OX5 ....17 G1
Churchill Wy RW/EYN OX29 ....6 B5
Church La ABGD OX14 ....62 C4
 HEAD OX3 ....27 F4
 KID OX5 ....35 G5
 KID OX5 ....11 H4
 KID OX5 ....16 D4
 RW/EYN OX29 ....23 G1
 WITNEY OX28 ....21 G3
Churchmere Rd ABGD OX14 ......63 G4
Church Mill Rd ABGD OX14 ....57 E4
Church Rd ABGD OX14 ....57 E4
 COW/LTMR OX4 ....46 A4
 MCHM/KBPZ OX13 ....46 A4
 RW/EYN OX29 ....6 B5
 RW/EYN OX29 ....12 E1
 RW/EYN OX29 ....9 G3
Church St ABGD OX14 ....63 G4
 KID OX5 ....10 B4
 MCHM/KBPZ OX13 ....58 C4
 RW/EYN OX29 ....22 C4
 WDSTK OX20 ....7 H5
Church Vw RW/EYN OX29 ....13 C1
Church View Rd WITNEY OX28 ..21 F4
Church Wk ABGD OX14 * 57 E4
 COW/LTMR OX4 ....33 F2
Church Wy COW/LTMR OX4 ......50 B1
 OXN/BOT/CM OX2 ....32 B5
Cinnamonta Rd ABGD OX14 ......42 C1
Circus St COW/LTMR OX4 ....32 B5
Clarendon Cl ABGD OX14 ....61 F2
Claymond Rd HEAD OX3 ....35 H2
Cleavers Sq COW/LTMR OX4 * ...51 H5
Cleveland Cl KID OX5 ....18 A1
Cleveland Dr COW/LTMR OX4 ...42 A5
Clevelands ABGD OX14 ....61 E1
Clifford Pl OXN/BOT/CM OX2 ...25 F3
Clifton Dr ABGD OX14 ....60 D2
Clinton Cl COW/LTMR OX4 ....51 H5
Clive Rd COW/LTMR OX4 ....42 B5
The Closes KID OX5 ....10 A4
Clover Cl OXN/BOT/CM OX2 .....38 D3
Clover Pl COW/LTMR OX4 ....51 H2
Clover Rd KID OX5 ....22 B4
Cobden Crs OX/KTN OX1 ....2 D6
Cockpit Cl WDSTK OX20 ....4 C4
Cogges La WHLY OX33 ....29 H4
Cogges Hill Rd WITNEY OX28 ....21 G4
Colemans Hl HEAD OX3 ....35 G3
Coleridge Cl COW/LTMR OX4 ....42 B4

Coleridge Dr ABGD OX14 60 B5
Colgrove Down
 OXN/BOT/CM OX2 38 C3
Collcutt Cl WHLY OX33 43 G3
College Cl WHLY OX33 37 H5
College La COW/LTMR OX4 50 D2
Colley Wd OX/KTN OX1 49 H2
Collice St KID OX5 11 H5
Collingwood Cl ABGD OX14 60 D1
Collins St COW/LTMR OX4 41 F1
Collinwood Cl HEAD OX3 35 H3
Collinwood Rd HEAD OX3 35 H3
Colterne Cl HEAD OX3 34 C1
Coltsfoot Sq COW/LTMR OX4 51 H3
Colwell Dr ABGD OX14 60 A3
 HEAD OX3 36 A2
 WITNEY OX28 20 D5
Combe Ga RW/EYN OX29 6 A1
Combe Rd OXN/BOT/CM OX2 2 A1
Combewell STAD OX44 52 C2
Comfrey Rd COW/LTMR OX4 51 H1
Common Cl RW/EYN OX29 12 B2
Common Rd RW/EYN OX29 12 B3
Compass Cl COW/LTMR OX4 42 A5
Complins Cl OXN/BOT/CM OX2 26 A5
Compton Dr ABGD OX14 56 B5
Compton Wy WITNEY OX28 21 G2
Conduit Rd ABGD OX14 60 C3
Conifer Cl OXN/BOT/CM OX2 39 E1
Coniston Av HEAD OX3 34 C2
Conway Rd MCHM/KBPZ OX13 55 F4
Conyer Cl KID OX5 11 G4
Conyger Cl KID OX5 11 G4
Coolidge Cl HEAD OX3 35 F5
Cooper Pl HEAD OX3 35 H3
Coopers Cl WHLY OX33 44 B1
Coopers La ABGD OX14 60 C4
Cope Cl OXN/BOT/CM OX2 39 F1
Copenhagen Dr ABGD OX14 60 B1
Coppock Cl HEAD OX3 35 G4
Copse La HEAD OX3 34 C2
The Copse ABGD OX14 61 G1
Copthorne Rd KID OX5 17 G1
Cordrey Gn COW/LTMR OX4 41 F5
Coriander Wy COW/LTMR OX4 51 H3
Corn Avill Cl ABGD OX14 56 C5
Corn Bar WITNEY OX28 20 D3
Corndel Gdns WITNEY OX28 21 E3
Corneville Rd ABGD OX14 62 B3
Cornfield Cl WITNEY OX28 20 C4
Cornmarket St OX/KTN OX1 2 E3
Corn St WITNEY OX28 21 E3
Cornwallis Rd COW/LTMR OX4 41 G4
Coromandel ABGD OX14 62 D1
Corunna Crs COW/LTMR OX4 42 C3
Cosin Cl COW/LTMR OX4 41 G1
Costar Cl COW/LTMR OX4 51 F1
Cothill Rd MCHM/KBPZ OX13 54 A3
Cotman Cl ABGD OX14 60 C5
Cotswold Crs HEAD OX3 34 A1
Cotswold Meadow
 WITNEY OX28 20 B4
Cotswold Rd OXN/BOT/CM OX2 38 D3
Cottesmore Rd COW/LTMR OX4 50 C2
Cotton Grass Cl
 COW/LTMR OX4 * 51 G3
County Pk WITNEY OX28 * 21 E5
Coupland Rd MCHM/KBPZ OX13 54 C1
Court Cl KID OX5 9 H5
Court Farm Rd COW/LTMR OX4 50 B1
Courtland Rd COW/LTMR OX4 41 G5
Court Place Gdns
 COW/LTMR OX4 50 B1
Courts Gdns WITNEY OX28 21 H2
The Court ABGD OX14 60 C1
Covent Cl ABGD OX14 56 B4
Coverley Rd HEAD OX3 42 B2
The Covert WDSTK OX20 5 E5
Cow La OX/KTN OX1 50 A3
Cowley Pl COW/LTMR OX4 3 H5
Cowley Rd COW/LTMR OX4 3 J5
 COW/LTMR OX4 50 D2
Cox's Gnd OXN/BOT/CM OX2 33 E1
Crabtree La ABGD OX14 62 B3
Crabtree Pl ABGD OX14 61 F3
Crabtree Rd OXN/BOT/CM OX2 39 F1
Cranbrook Ct WITNEY OX28 * 21 E5
Cranbrook Dr OX/KTN OX1 50 A5
Cranesbill Wy COW/LTMR OX4 51 G3
Cranham St OXN/BOT/CM OX2 2 B1
Cranham Ter OXN/BOT/CM OX2 33 F3
Cranley Rd HEAD OX3 35 H2
Cranmer Rd COW/LTMR OX4 42 C3
Craufurd Rd COW/LTMR OX4 42 C3
Crawley Rd WITNEY OX28 21 E1
Crecy Wk WDSTK OX20 5 E5
Crescent Cl COW/LTMR OX4 42 B3
Crescent Rd COW/LTMR OX4 42 A3
The Crescent COW/LTMR OX4 51 E4
 WITNEY OX28 21 G1
Cress Hill Pl HEAD OX3 35 H2
Cricket Rd COW/LTMR OX4 41 G2
Crick Rd OXN/BOT/CM OX2 33 G2
Cripley Pl OXN/BOT/CM OX2 2 A3
Cripley Rd OXN/BOT/CM OX2 2 A3
Croasdell Cl ABGD OX14 63 E1
The Croft HEAD OX3 35 F3
Croft Av KID OX5 10 B5
Croft Cl HEAD OX3 34 B2
Croft Rd HEAD OX3 34 B2
The Crofts WITNEY OX28 21 E4
Cromwell Cl HEAD OX3 34 A2
Cromwell Pl WHLY OX33 * 45 E1
Cromwell St OX/KTN OX1 2 E5
Cromwell Wy KID OX5 17 H2
Crosslands Dr ABGD OX14 60 B1
Cross St COW/LTMR OX4 3 K5
Crotch Crs HEAD OX3 34 C2
Crowberry Rd COW/LTMR OX4 51 H2
Crowell Rd COW/LTMR OX4 42 A5
Crown Ms ABGD OX14 * 60 C3
Crown Rd KID OX5 9 H5
 WHLY OX33 44 D1
Crown St COW/LTMR OX4 41 F1
Croxford Gdns KID OX5 17 G2
Crozier Cl OXN/BOT/CM OX2 39 F1
Cuckamus La RW/EYN OX29 12 B2
Cuckoo La RW/EYN OX29 13 F2
Cuddesdon Rd WHLY OX33 43 G3
Cuddesdon Wy COW/LTMR OX4 51 G2
Culham Cl ABGD OX14 61 E1
Cullerne Cl ABGD OX14 56 A4
Cullum Rd WHLY OX33 45 E1
Cumberland Rd COW/LTMR OX4 41 H2
Cumberlege Cl HEAD OX3 27 E4
Cummings Cl HEAD OX3 35 G4
Cumnor Hl OXN/BOT/CM OX2 38 B4
Cumnor Rise Rd
 OXN/BOT/CM OX2 39 E1
Cumnor Rd OX/KTN OX1 47 G3
 OXN/BOT/CM OX2 30 C5
Cunliffe Cl OXN/BOT/CM OX2 26 B5
Curbridge Rd RW/EYN OX29 20 B5
Curtis Av ABGD OX14 61 F3
Curtis Rd KID OX5 10 A4
Curtyn Cl ABGD OX14 60 B2
Cygnet Ct ABGD OX14 60 C4

D

Daisy Bank ABGD OX14 61 F2
Dale Cl OX/KTN OX1 2 C6
Danvers Rd COW/LTMR OX4 50 C1
Darell Wy ABGD OX14 60 D1
Dark La MCHM/KBPZ OX13 55 G2
 WITNEY OX28 21 E2
Dart Rd MCHM/KBPZ OX13 55 E4
Dashwood Av KID OX5 16 D3
Dashwood Rd COW/LTMR OX4 50 C1
Daubeny Rd COW/LTMR OX4 41 F3
Davenant Rd OXN/BOT/CM OX2 26 A3
Davenport Rd WITNEY OX28 20 D2
David Nicholls Cl
 COW/LTMR OX4 50 D2
David Walter Cl
 OXN/BOT/CM OX2 26 B2
Dawson Pl OXN/BOT/CM OX2 * 2 A1
Dawson St COW/LTMR OX4 3 J5
Dean Court Rd
 OXN/BOT/CM OX2 38 D2
Deanfield Rd OXN/BOT/CM OX2 31 H5
Dearlove Cl ABGD OX14 55 G5
Deaufort Cl KID OX5 10 A4
Deer Park Rd WITNEY OX28 20 B3
Delamare Wy OXN/BOT/CM OX2 38 D2
Delawarr Ct OXN/BOT/CM OX2 39 G2
Delbush Av HEAD OX3 36 B2
Demesne Furze HEAD OX3 34 D5
Dene Ri WITNEY OX28 20 D3
Dene Rd HEAD OX3 42 B1
Denman's La OXN/BOT/CM OX2 38 A4
Denmark St COW/LTMR OX4 3 K6
Denton Cl ABGD OX14 61 F2
 OXN/BOT/CM OX2 38 C1
Denton Hl STAD OX44 53 H3
Denton La STAD OX44 53 E3
Dents Cl HEAD OX3 34 C1
Derwent Av HEAD OX3 34 C2
Derwent Cl MCHM/KBPZ OX13 55 E5
Desborough Crs
 COW/LTMR OX4 50 B1
Devereux Pl COW/LTMR OX4 50 D1
Diamond Pl OXN/BOT/CM OX2 26 B5
Didcot Rd ABGD OX14 65 H5
Divinity Rd COW/LTMR OX4 41 G1
Dodgson Rd COW/LTMR OX4 42 A5
Dodson Ct ABGD OX14 60 D3
Don Boscoe Cl COW/LTMR OX4 42 B3
Donnington Bridge Rd
 COW/LTMR OX4 41 F4
Donnington Cl WITNEY OX28 20 B4
Don Stuart Pl COW/LTMR OX4 41 H2
Dora Carr Cl HEAD OX3 34 C1
Dorchester Cl HEAD OX3 35 H5
Dorchester Crs ABGD OX14 61 E1
Doris Field Cl HEAD OX3 34 B3
Dove House Cl
 OXN/BOT/CM OX2 25 H3
Dovehouse Cl RW/EYN OX29 22 D3
Down Cl COW/LTMR OX4 51 G4
Downside End HEAD OX3 36 A3
Downside Rd HEAD OX3 35 H3
Doyley Rd OXN/BOT/CM OX2 40 A1
Drayton East Wy ABGD OX14 62 C5
Drayton Rd ABGD OX14 62 D4
 ABGD OX14 62 C2
Drove Acre Rd COW/LTMR OX4 41 G2
Druce Wy COW/LTMR OX4 51 H1
Dry La RW/EYN OX29 20 B1
Drysdale Cl ABGD OX14 57 E5
Ducklington La WITNEY OX28 20 D4
Dudgeon Dr COW/LTMR OX4 50 D2
Duffield Cl ABGD OX14 56 B5
Duffield Pl MCHM/KBPZ OX13 58 C3
Dukes Rd KID OX5 10 B5
Duke St OXN/BOT/CM OX2 32 D5
Duncan Cl RW/EYN OX29 22 B3
Dundas Cl ABGD OX14 61 F2
Dunmore Rd ABGD OX14 55 G5
Dunnock Wy COW/LTMR OX4 51 G3
Dunstan Rd HEAD OX3 35 E2
Dynham Pl HEAD OX3 35 F5

E

Earl St OXN/BOT/CM OX2 32 D5
Early Rd WITNEY OX28 21 G1
Eason Dr ABGD OX14 61 G1
East Av COW/LTMR OX4 41 G1
Eastchurch COW/LTMR OX4 50 B1
Eastern Av COW/LTMR OX4 50 D1
Eastern By-Pass Rd
 COW/LTMR OX4 42 C4
 HEAD OX3 35 H3
East Field Cl HEAD OX3 42 C2
Eastfield Rd WITNEY OX28 21 F1
East Saint Helen St ABGD OX14 60 D4
East St OXN/BOT/CM OX2 2 A4
East Wy ABGD OX14 62 B5
Eastwood Rd RW/EYN OX29 20 A2
Eaton Rd MCHM/KBPZ OX13 46 A5
Eden Cft ABGD OX14 56 A5
Eden Dr HEAD OX3 34 C2
Edgecombe Rd HEAD OX3 35 G2
Edgeway Rd HEAD OX3 34 B3
Edinburgh Dr KID OX5 10 C5
Edington Rd WITNEY OX28 20 B3
Edith Rd OX/KTN OX1 40 C3
Edmund Halley Rd
 COW/LTMR OX4 50 D3
Edmund Rd COW/LTMR OX4 42 A4
Edward Rd OX/KTN OX1 50 A3
Edward St ABGD OX14 60 B3
Egerton Rd COW/LTMR OX4 41 G5
Elder Wy COW/LTMR OX4 51 H3
Eldridge Cl ABGD OX14 55 H5
Eleanor Cl COW/LTMR OX4 41 H5
Electric Av OXN/BOT/CM OX2 40 A1
Elizabeth Av ABGD OX14 56 C5
Elizabeth Jennings Wy
 OXN/BOT/CM OX2 26 A5
Ellesmere Rd COW/LTMR OX4 41 G5
Elm Cl WHLY OX33 45 E2
 WITNEY OX28 20 C3
Elm Dr STAD OX44 52 C2
Elm Gv KID OX5 17 H2
Elms Dr HEAD OX3 34 B1
Elms Pde OXN/BOT/CM OX2 32 B5
Elms Rd OXN/BOT/CM OX2 32 A5
 RW/EYN OX29 23 G1
Elmthorpe Rd
 OXN/BOT/CM OX2 25 G3
Elm Tree Cl COW/LTMR OX4 50 D1
Elm Tree Wk MCHM/KBPZ OX13 59 H1
Elsfield Rd HEAD OX3 27 F5
Elsfield Wy OXN/BOT/CM OX2 26 B2
Elton Cl HEAD OX3 36 B2
Elton Crs WHLY OX33 45 E2
Elwes Cl ABGD OX14 61 F2
Elwes Rd MCHM/KBPZ OX13 58 D3
Ely Cl ABGD OX14 60 A4
Emperor Gdns COW/LTMR OX4 51 G3
Eney Cl ABGD OX14 56 C5
Erica Cl COW/LTMR OX4 51 H2
Essex St COW/LTMR OX4 41 G2
Ethelhelm Cl ABGD OX14 56 B4
Ethelred Ct HEAD OX3 35 E2
Eton Cl WITNEY OX28 21 H4
Evans Cl RW/EYN OX29 22 C3
Evans Ct KID OX5 10 B5
Evans La KID OX5 10 B5
Evans Rd RW/EYN OX29 22 C4
Evelin Rd ABGD OX14 60 C1
Evelyn Cl OXN/BOT/CM OX2 38 D1
Evenlode Cl RW/EYN OX29 12 B2
Evenlode Crs KID OX5 9 E3
Evenlode Dr RW/EYN OX29 6 A4
Evenlode Pk ABGD OX14 61 F1
Everard Cl HEAD OX3 35 F5
Ewert Pl OXN/BOT/CM OX2 26 B5
Ewin Cl HEAD OX3 34 B1
Exbourne Rd ABGD OX14 60 B3
Exeter Rd KID OX5 10 A4
Eynsham Rd OXN/BOT/CM OX2 30 D4
 RW/EYN OX29 23 G2
Eyot Pl COW/LTMR OX4 41 E2
Eyston Wy ABGD OX14 60 A3

F

Faber Cl COW/LTMR OX4 51 E2
Fairacres ABGD OX14 59 H3
Fairacres Rd COW/LTMR OX4 41 F3
Fairfax Av HEAD OX3 34 A2
Fairfax Rd COW/LTMR OX4 42 C3
 KID OX5 17 H2
Fairfield Dr WITNEY OX28 20 D4
Fairfield Pl ABGD OX14 60 D2
Fairlawn End OXN/BOT/CM OX2 25 H3
Fairlawn Whf ABGD OX14 60 D4
Fairlie Rd COW/LTMR OX4 50 D1
Fair Vw HEAD OX3 42 B2
Falcon Cl COW/LTMR OX4 51 F2
Fallowfield Crs RW/EYN OX29 21 H2
Falstaff Cl RW/EYN OX29 22 B3
Fane Rd HEAD OX3 34 A1
Fanshawe Pl COW/LTMR OX4 42 C4
Faringdon Rd ABGD OX14 60 C2
 MCHM/KBPZ OX13 59 F1
 OXN/BOT/CM OX2 47 E1
Farm Cl COW/LTMR OX4 51 H3
 KID OX5 10 A4
Farm Close La WHLY OX33 44 D1
Farm Close Rd WHLY OX33 44 D1
Farmer Pl HEAD OX3 34 B2
Farmers Cl WITNEY OX28 21 F1
Farmhouse Meadow
 WITNEY OX28 20 C5
Farmington Dr
 WITNEY OX28 20 C3
Farm Mill La WITNEY OX28 21 F4
Farmoor Ct OXN/BOT/CM OX2 30 C4
Farm Rd ABGD OX14 55 H5
Farndon Rd OXN/BOT/CM OX2 33 F2
The Farthings
 MCHM/KBPZ OX13 58 C4
Faulkner St OX/KTN OX1 2 D5
Fenlock Rd RW/EYN OX29 7 F4
Fennel Wy ABGD OX14 61 G2
Ferguson Pl ABGD OX14 61 G2
Fernhill Cl KID OX5 9 H5
Fern Hill Rd COW/LTMR OX4 42 B4
Fernhill Rd KID OX5 9 E5
Ferny Cl ABGD OX14 57 E4
Ferry Hinksey Rd
 OXN/BOT/CM OX2 33 E5
Ferry Pool Rd
 OXN/BOT/CM OX2 26 B5
Ferry Rd HEAD OX3 34 A3
Ferry Wk ABGD OX14 60 D5
Fettiplace Cl MCHM/KBPZ OX13 46 A5
Fettiplace Rd HEAD OX3 35 G1
 MCHM/KBPZ OX13 58 D3
 WITNEY OX28 20 C3
Field Av COW/LTMR OX4 51 H3
Field Cl KID OX5 10 B5
 KID OX5 16 D2
Fielden Gv HEAD OX3 34 C3
Fieldfare Rd COW/LTMR OX4 51 G4
Field House Dr
 OXN/BOT/CM OX2 26 A3
Fieldmere Cl WITNEY OX28 20 C3
Fieldside ABGD OX14 60 B1
 ABGD OX14 65 H5
The Field MCHM/KBPZ OX13 54 B1
Fiennes Rd COW/LTMR OX4 50 C1
Finch Cl HEAD OX3 35 E4
Finmore Cl ABGD OX14 60 C2
Finmore Rd OXN/BOT/CM OX2 39 F1
Firs Meadow
 COW/LTMR OX4 51 G4
First Turn OXN/BOT/CM OX2 25 H3
Fir Trees OX/KTN OX1 50 A5
Fisher Cl ABGD OX14 62 A4
Fisherman's Whf ABGD OX14 63 F1
Fitchett Yd ABGD OX14 60 C3
Fitzharry's Rd ABGD OX14 60 D2
Fitzherbert Cl COW/LTMR OX4 41 F5
Five Mile Dr OXN/BOT/CM OX2 26 A2
Flatford Pl KID OX5 9 G3
Flaxfield Rd COW/LTMR OX4 51 H2
Flemings Rd WDSTK OX20 5 E4
Fletcher Cl KID OX5 16 D3
Fletcher Rd COW/LTMR OX4 42 C3
Flexney Pl HEAD OX3 35 F5
Florence Cl KID OX5 10 A5
Florence Park Rd
 COW/LTMR OX4 41 H4
Floyd's Rw OX/KTN OX1 2 E5
Fogwell Rd
 OXN/BOT/CM OX2 38 C1
Folly Br OX/KTN OX1 2 E6
Ford La MCHM/KBPZ OX13 58 A3
Fords Cl WHLY OX33 43 G3
Forest Rd HEAD OX3 35 H3
Forest Side OX/KTN OX1 49 H1
Forget-me-not Wy
 COW/LTMR OX4 51 G3
Forster La OXN/BOT/CM OX2 38 A5
Fortnam Cl HEAD OX3 34 D3
Foster Rd ABGD OX14 55 H4
Fountain Ct ABGD OX14 61 E2
Foxborough Rd ABGD OX14 57 E5
Fox Cl STAD OX44 52 D2
Foxcombe La OX/KTN OX1 49 E3
Foxcombe Rd OX/KTN OX1 49 E2
Fox Crs OX/KTN OX1 41 E4
Foxdown Cl KID OX5 10 A4
Fox Furlong COW/LTMR OX4 50 C3
Foxglove Cl COW/LTMR OX4 51 G3
Foxglove Rd KID OX5 9 F5
Fox La MCHM/KBPZ OX13 55 E1
Foxton Cl OXN/BOT/CM OX2 25 H2
Foxwell Dr HEAD OX3 34 D1
Francis Little Dr ABGD OX14 60 B5
Franklin Cl KID OX5 10 B4
Franklin Rd HEAD OX3 34 D3
Franklyn Cl ABGD OX14 55 H5
Frederick Rd COW/LTMR OX4 42 B5
Freeborn Cl KID OX5 10 A3
Freelands Rd COW/LTMR OX4 41 F4
Frenchay Rd OXN/BOT/CM OX2 33 E1
French Cl WITNEY OX28 20 D4
Frewin Ct OX/KTN OX1 2 D3
Friars Entry OX/KTN OX1 2 D3
Friars Whf OX/KTN OX1 2 D6
Friday La WHLY OX33 44 D1
Frieze Wy KID OX5 17 H3
Frilford Rd MCHM/KBPZ OX13 58 B4
Fruitlands RW/EYN OX29 22 A3
Frys Hl COW/LTMR OX4 51 G4
Fullwell Cl ABGD OX14 60 C1
Furlong Cl COW/LTMR OX4 51 F1
Fyfield Rd OXN/BOT/CM OX2 33 G2

G

Gainsborough Gn ABGD OX14 60 B5
Gaisford Rd COW/LTMR OX4 42 A5
Gall Cl ABGD OX14 61 G2
Galley Fld ABGD OX14 61 F2
Galpin Cl COW/LTMR OX4 41 G2
The Gap MCHM/KBPZ OX13 58 C4
The Gardens ABGD OX14 57 E4
Gardiner Cl ABGD OX14 61 G2
 WHLY OX33 37 G5
Gardiner St HEAD OX3 35 F4
Garford Cl ABGD OX14 56 B5
Garford Rd OXN/BOT/CM OX2 33 G1
Garsington Rd COW/LTMR OX4 42 B4
The Garth KID OX5 16 D3
 OXN/BOT/CM OX2 39 F1
Gathorne Rd HEAD OX3 35 F4
Gentian Rd COW/LTMR OX4 51 H2
Geoffrey Barbour Rd
 ABGD OX14 60 D2
George Moore Cl
 COW/LTMR OX4 4
George St OX/KTN OX1 2
George Street Ms OX/KTN OX1 2
Gerard Pl COW/LTMR OX4 42
Gibbs Crs OXN/BOT/CM OX2 2
Gibson Cl ABGD OX14 5
Gidley Wy WHLY OX33 44
Giles Cl COW/LTMR OX4 5
Giles Rd COW/LTMR OX4 5
Gillians Wy COW/LTMR OX4 4
Ginge Cl ABGD OX14 5
Gipsy La HEAD OX3 34
Girdlestone Rd HEAD OX3 3
Gladstone Rd HEAD OX3 3
Glanville Rd COW/LTMR OX4 41
Glebelands HEAD OX3 42
Glebe Rd OXN/BOT/CM OX2 38
Glebe St COW/LTMR OX4 3
The Glebe ABGD OX14 63
 OXN/BOT/CM OX2 38
 WHLY OX33 44
Gloucester Gn OX/KTN OX1 2
Gloucester La OX/KTN OX1 2
Gloucester Pl WITNEY OX28 21
Gloucester St OX/KTN OX1 2
Glovers Cl WDSTK OX20 5
Glyme Cl ABGD OX14 61
 WDSTK OX20 4
Glyme Wy RW/EYN OX29 6
Godfrey Cl ABGD OX14 60
 HEAD OX3 35
Godstow Rd OXN/BOT/CM OX2 25
Godwyn Cl ABGD OX14 60
Golafre Rd ABGD OX14 60
Golden Rd COW/LTMR OX4 41
Goodson Wk HEAD OX3 34
Gooseacre ABGD OX14 57
Gordon Cl HEAD OX3 34
Gordon Dr ABGD OX14 61
Gordon St OX/KTN OX1 40
Gordon Wy WITNEY OX28 21
Gorse Leas HEAD OX3 34
Gosford Cl KID OX5 17
Goslyn Cl HEAD OX3 35
Gouldland Gdns HEAD OX3 34
Grand Br WDSTK OX20 4
Grange Ct OXN/BOT/CM OX2 31
Grange Rd COW/LTMR OX4 50
Grants Ms COW/LTMR OX4 3
The Grates COW/LTMR OX4 42
Gravel La ABGD OX14 62
Gravel Pits La KID OX5 16
Grays Rd HEAD OX3 34
Great Clarendon St
 OXN/BOT/CM OX2 2
Great Close Rd KID OX5 16
Great Md OXN/BOT/CM OX2 2
Grebe Cl ABGD OX14 60
Greenacres ABGD OX14 62
Green Close Goose
 OXN/BOT/CM OX2 25
Greenfinch Cl COW/LTMR OX4 51
Green Hl COW/LTMR OX4 52
Green La MCHM/KBPZ OX13 54
 MCHM/KBPZ OX13 56
 OXN/BOT/CM OX2 38
 WDSTK OX20 4
Green Pl OX/KTN OX1 40
Green Ridges HEAD OX3 36
Green Rd HEAD OX3 35
 KID OX5 10
Green's Rd RW/EYN OX29 22
Green St COW/LTMR OX4 41
The Green RW/EYN OX29 23
 STAD OX44 53
 WDSTK OX20 7
Grenoble Rd COW/LTMR OX4 51
Greystones Ct KID OX5 9
Grosvenor Rd
 OXN/BOT/CM OX2 39
Grovelands KID OX5 9
Grovelands Rd HEAD OX3 36
Grove Rd WDSTK OX20 8
Grove St OXN/BOT/CM OX2 26
The Grove ABGD OX14 56
Grundy Cl ABGD OX14 61
Grundy Crs OX/KTN OX1 50
Grunsell Cl HEAD OX3 34
Guelder Rd COW/LTMR OX4 51
Gurden Pl HEAD OX3 35
Guri Cl HEAD OX3 35
Gwyneth Rd COW/LTMR OX4 50

H

Hadland Rd ABGD OX14 61
Hadow Rd HEAD OX3 34
Haines Ct MCHM/KBPZ OX13 58
Haldane Rd COW/LTMR OX4 51
Halliday Hl HEAD OX3 34
Halls Cl ABGD OX14 62
 OXN/BOT/CM OX2 39
Hamble Dr ABGD OX14 61
Hamels La OX/KTN OX1 48
The Hamel OX/KTN OX1 * 2
Hamilton Rd OXN/BOT/CM OX2 26
Hampden Dr KID OX5 17
Hampden Rd COW/LTMR OX4 42
Hanborough Cl RW/EYN OX29 22
Hanborough Rd RW/EYN OX29 22
Handlo Pl HEAD OX3 35
Hanson Rd ABGD OX14 55
Harberton Md HEAD OX3 34
Harbord Rd OXN/BOT/CM OX2 26
Harcourt Hl OXN/BOT/CM OX2 39
Harcourt Ter HEAD OX3 34
Harcourt Wy ABGD OX14 60
Harding Rd ABGD OX14 60

ngs Cl COW/LTMR OX4 ......50 D1
wick Av KID OX5 ......17 G1
ell Rd COW/LTMR OX4 ......51 H2
ields OXN/BOT/CM OX2 ......26 B2
w Wy HEAD OX3 ......35 F3
de Cl HEAD OX3 ......35 F2
d Hicks Pl COW/LTMR OX4 ..41 F3
d White Cl HEAD OX3 * 35 H4
es Rd COW/LTMR OX4 ......51 H1
sichord Pl COW/LTMR OX4 ..3 K4
son's La WDSTK OX20 ......4 C4
w Rd COW/LTMR OX4 ......51 H1
l ABGD OX14 ......61 G2
Cl KID OX5 ......2 B1
st OXN/BOT/CM OX2 ......2 B1
est Wy RW/EYN OX29 ......21 H1
ell Cl ABGD OX14 ......61 E1
e Gra HEAD OX3 ......34 C2
aways WHLY OX33 ......44 D1
lock Rd COW/LTMR OX4 ......42 A4
ins St COW/LTMR OX4 ......3 G1
kins Wy MCHM/KBPZ OX13 ..54 D1
ksmoor Rd
  OXN/BOT/CM OX2 ......26 B2
kswell Gdns
thorn Av HEAD OX3 ......26 C4
thorne Av
  CHM/KBPZ OX13 ......59 H1
thorne Cl
thorn Rd RW/EYN OX29 ......22 C3
es Cl HEAD OX3 ......17 G1
eld Rd OXN/BOT/CM OX2 ..33 F1
es Rd HEAD OX3 ......35 F3
ward Rd OXN/BOT/CM OX2 ..26 A1
wards Rd ABGD OX14 ......62 B5
ers KID OX5 ......17 G2
inut Pth OX/KTN OX1 ......50 A5
red Wy KID OX5 ......17 G1
es Cl HEAD OX3 ......34 C4
llington HI HEAD OX3 ......34 C4
lley Wy HEAD OX3 ......34 D3
ley Cl ABGD OX14 ......60 C5
es Cl HEAD OX3 ......42 B1
hcote P HEAD OX3 ......61 G1
ther Pl HEAD OX3 ......34 B2
e End WDSTK OX20 ......5 E5
jemead Av HEAD OX3 ......61 G1
nd OXN/BOT/CM OX2 ......32 D5
ys Pl KID OX5 ......9 H3
dred St COW/LTMR OX4 ..41 H4
dred Wy HEAD OX3 ......61 F1
grove Cl HEAD OX3 ......35 F2
ey Av COW/LTMR OX4 ......41 G4
ey Rd COW/LTMR OX4 ......50 D4
eys La ABGD OX14 ......62 B4
ey St COW/LTMR OX4 ......3 K7
or Mill Cl ABGD OX14 ......56 B5
ry Box Cl WITNEY OX28 ..21 E4
ry Rd OXN/BOT/CM OX2 ..33 E5
ry Taunt Cl HEAD OX3 ......35 H5
sington Cl WDSTK OX20 ....5 E5
sington Rd WDSTK OX20 ....4 C4
wood Dr OX/KTN OX1 ......47 G3
pert Cl COW/LTMR OX4 ......3 G1
man Cl ABGD OX14 ......61 F2
mitage Rd ABGD OX14 ......60 B4
mes Rd COW/LTMR OX4 ..26 B3
on Ct ABGD OX14 ......60 D1
on's Wk ABGD OX14 ......60 D1
schel Crs COW/LTMR OX4 ..51 E1
tford St COW/LTMR OX4 ....41 G2
croft RW/EYN OX29 ......22 C2
ford Hill La COW/LTMR OX4 .50 B2
ford Rd KID OX5 ......9 H4
s Copse Rd
  OXN/BOT/CM OX2 ......38 C2
l Cross Wy HEAD OX3 ......35 H4
nfield Av HEAD OX3 ......35 H4
n St ABGD OX14 ......60 D3
worth Pl WITNEY OX28 ....21 F2
n Rd WHLY OX33 ......45 E2
craft Rd WHLY OX33 ......45 E2
st Flds ABGD OX14 ......62 A5
ers Cl ABGD OX14 ......63 F5
ari WDSTK OX20 ......5 E4
  WHLY OX33 ......43 H3
sborough Rd 41 H5
side OXN/BOT/CM OX2 ......38 C3
ill STAD OX44 ......53 H4
top Gdns KID OX5 ......11 H4
Top Rd COW/LTMR OX4 ......26 B4
w La 36 A2
View La MCHM/KBPZ OX13 ..44 D4
view Rd ABGD OX14 ......60 D4
  OXN/BOT/CM OX2 ......33 E5
ksey HI HEAD OX3 ......49 F1
Ms ABGD OX14 ......60 D4
s Wd KID OX5 ......11 H3
iby Cl COW/LTMR OX4 ......61 H3
son Rd OXN/BOT/CM OX2 ..26 B4
ckmore St COW/LTMR OX4 ..42 A5
ges Ct OX/KTN OX1 ......2 E7
garth Pl ABGD OX14 ......47 H1
ford Rd WITNEY OX28 ......20 D4
land St ABGD OX14 ......42 C1
land Rd HEAD OX3 ......55 H5
ey Crs HEAD OX3 ......35 F3

Hollis Cl WITNEY OX28 ......21 H4
Holloway Rd WHLY OX33 ......44 D1
  WITNEY OX28 ......21 E8
Hollow Furlong RW/EYN OX29 ..3 G1
Hollybush Rw OX/KTN OX1 ......2 B4
The Holt ABGD OX14 ......60 D2
Holy Cl KID OX5 ......17 G1
Holyoake Rd HEAD OX3 ......35 F3
Holywell Cl ABGD OX14 ......56 C5
Holywell St OX/KTN OX1 ......3 F2
Home Cl KID OX5 ......10 A4
  MCHM/KBPZ OX13 ......47 H5
  MCHM/KBPZ OX13 ......54 D1
  OXN/BOT/CM OX2 ......25 D2
Homestall Cl OXN/BOT/CM OX2 .31 H5
The Homestead KID OX5 ......9 H5
  WDSTK OX20 ......8 A2
Honeybottom La
  WDSTK OX20 ......9 H5
Honeysuckle Gv
  COW/LTMR OX4 * 52 A2
Honor Cl KID OX5 ......10 B5
Hornbeam Dr COW/LTMR OX4 ..52 A2
Horseman Cl HEAD OX3 ......34 B1
Horsemere Cl RW/EYN OX29 ..23 H1
Horseshoes Cl
  MCHM/KBPZ OX13 ......46 A5
Horspath Driftway HEAD OX3 ..42 C2
Horspath Rd COW/LTMR OX4 ..42 B3
Horwood Cl HEAD OX3 ......35 E3
Hosker Cl HEAD OX3 ......36 A2
Hound Cl ABGD OX14 ......60 C5
Howard Cornish Rd 58 D3
Howard St COW/LTMR OX4 ....41 F3
Howe Cl WHLY OX33 ......44 D1
Hugh Allen Crs HEAD OX3 ......34 B5
Humfrey Rd HEAD OX3 ......35 H2
Hundred Acres Cl HEAD OX3 ..34 B5
Hunsdon Rd COW/LTMR OX4 ..33 H5
Hunter Cl ABGD OX14 ......56 B4
  COW/LTMR OX4 ......42 C3
Hurdeswell RW/EYN OX29 ......6 A4
Hurst La COW/LTMR OX4 ......38 D5
  RW/EYN OX29 ......13 C2
Hurst Rise Rd OXN/BOT/CM OX2 .39 E1
Hurst St COW/LTMR OX4 ......3 K7
Hutchcombe Farm Cl
  OXN/BOT/CM OX2 ......39 E1
Hutchcomb Rd
Huxley Cl COW/LTMR OX4 ......39 E1
Hyacinth Wk COW/LTMR OX4 ..51 C4
Hyde Copse MCHM/KBPZ OX13 .58 D4
Hyde Pl ABGD OX14 ......60 B5
The Hyde ABGD OX14 ......60 B5
Hythe Bridge St OX/KTN OX1 ..2 B3

I

Idbury Cl WITNEY OX28 ......20 B4
Iffley Cl COW/LTMR OX4 ......3 J6
Iffley Turn COW/LTMR OX4 ......3 J6
Ilsley Rd HEAD OX3 ......35 C2
Ingle Cl HEAD OX3 ......34 D2
Inkerman Cl ABGD OX14 ......60 B5
Inott Furze HEAD OX3 ......42 B2
Isis Cl ABGD OX14 ......61 F1
  RW/EYN OX29 ......6 B5
Islip Rd OXN/BOT/CM OX2 ......26 B5

J

Jack Argent Cl COW/LTMR OX4 * 51 H3
Jackdaw La COW/LTMR OX4 ....41 E2
Jackies La WHLY OX33 ......45 E2
Jackman Cl ABGD OX14 ......61 E3
Jackson Dr OX/KTN OX1 ......49 H2
Jackson Rd OXN/BOT/CM OX2 ..26 B3
Jacobs Cl WITNEY OX28 ......21 F2
James St COW/LTMR OX4 ......3 K6
James Wolfe Rd HEAD OX3 ......42 C2
Janaway Pl COW/LTMR OX4 ....50 C3
Jarn Wy OX/KTN OX1 ......48 B3
Jasmine Ct COW/LTMR OX4 ....51 H2
Jericho St COW/LTMR OX4 ......2 B1
Jersey Rd COW/LTMR OX4 ......50 C1
Jeune St COW/LTMR OX4 ......3 K4
Joan Lawrence Pl HEAD OX3 ..35 C5
John Buchan Rd HEAD OX3 ....34 D1
John Garne Wy HEAD OX3 ......35 F5
John Lopes Rd RW/EYN OX29 ..22 C4
John Mason Rd ABGD OX14 ....61 E2
John Morris Rd ABGD OX14 ....60 C5
John Snow Pl HEAD OX3 ......35 C3
John Towle Cl OX/KTN OX1 ....40 C4
Jordan HI OXN/BOT/CM OX2 ..26 A1
Jourdain Rd COW/LTMR OX4 ..51 H1
Jowett Wk COW/LTMR OX4 ......3 G2
Jubilee Ter COW/LTMR OX4 ......2 D6
Jubilee Wy RW/EYN OX29 ......21 H2
Judd's Cl WITNEY OX28 ......21 H3
Judges Cl KID OX5 ......9 H5
Junction Rd COW/LTMR OX4 ..42 B3
Juniper Dr COW/LTMR OX4 ......51 H2
Juxon St OXN/BOT/CM OX2 ......33 E3

K

Kames Cl COW/LTMR OX4 ......41 H4
Keble Rd OX/KTN OX1 ......2 D1
Keene Cl COW/LTMR OX4 ......50 D4
Kelburne Rd COW/LTMR OX4 ..41 H5
Kelham Hall Dr WHLY OX33 ....44 D2
Kelly's Rd WHLY OX33 ......44 D2
Kempson Crs COW/LTMR OX4 ..50 C2
Kempster Cl ABGD OX14 ......61 F2
Kendall Crs COW/LTMR OX4 ..26 B4
Kenilworth Av COW/LTMR OX4 .41 H2
Kenilworth Rd 38 A5
Kennedy Cl HEAD OX3 ......42 C2
Kennett Rd ABGD OX14 ......61 F1
Kennett Rd HEAD OX3 ......35 E3
Kennington Rd ABGD OX14 ....57 E2
  OX/KTN OX1 ......50 A2
Kensington Cl ABGD OX14 ......63 E1
Kent Cl ABGD OX14 ......50 A5
  COW/LTMR OX4 ......51 G1
Kenville Rd COW/LTMR OX4 ..49 H2
Kersington Crs COW/LTMR OX4 .51 F1
Kerwood Cl WDSTK OX20 ......4 D3
Kestrel Crs COW/LTMR OX4 ..51 F2
Kestrel Rd MCHM/KBPZ OX13 .54 D5
Keydale Rd WHLY OX33 ......44 B1
Kidlington Rd KID OX5 ......11 G4
Kiln Cl HEAD OX3 ......50 D4
Kiln La HEAD OX3 ......35 H4
  STAD OX44 ......53 C2
  WHLY OX33 ......44 C1
Kimber Cl WHLY OX33 ......44 C1
Kimber Rd ABGD OX14 ......59 H5
Kineton Rd OX/KTN OX1 ......40 C2
King Edward St COW/LTMR OX4 .3 F4
Kingfisher Cl ABGD OX14 ......63 F1
Kingfisher Dr WITNEY OX28 ..21 H5
Kingfisher Gn COW/LTMR OX4 .51 H5
Kings Av MCHM/KBPZ OX13 ..58 C5
King's Cross Rd
  OXN/BOT/CM OX2 ......26 B4
Kingsfield Crs WITNEY OX28 ..21 G3
Kingsgate COW/LTMR OX4 * ..42 B5
King's Head La KID OX5 ......11 H4
King's Mill La HEAD OX3 ......35 H5
Kingston Cl ABGD OX14 ......60 D2
Kingston Hts RW/EYN OX29 ..33 F2
Kingston Rd OXN/BOT/CM OX2 .33 E2
King St OXN/BOT/CM OX2 ......33 E3
Kings Way Dr KID OX5 ......10 C5
Kirby Pl COW/LTMR OX4 ......42 C4
Kirk Cl OX/KTN OX1 ......50 A4
  OXN/BOT/CM OX2 ......26 A2
Knapp Cl ABGD OX14 ......60 B5
Knights Rd COW/LTMR OX4 ....51 F2
Knolles Rd COW/LTMR OX4 ..42 A4
Knollys Cl ABGD OX14 ......56 A4
Kybald St OX/KTN OX1 ......3 G4
Kysbie Cl ABGD OX14 ......55 H5

L

Laburnam Av
  MCHM/KBPZ OX13 ......60 A1
Laburnum Crs KID OX5 ......17 G2
Laburnum Rd
  OXN/BOT/CM OX2 ......39 F2
Ladder HI WHLY OX33 ......44 C2
Ladenham Rd COW/LTMR OX4 .51 G1
Lady Eleanor Ct ABGD OX14 ..60 B5
Ladygrove Ct ABGD OX14 ......60 B5
Ladygrove Paddock ABGD OX14 .60 B4
Ladywell Cl COW/LTMR OX4 ..51 C2
Lakefield Rd COW/LTMR OX4 ..51 G2
Lakeside OXN/BOT/CM OX2 ..25 H1
Lakesmere Cl KID OX5 ......9 H3
Lake St OX/KTN OX1 ......40 C2
Lamarsh Rd OXN/BOT/CM OX2 .32 C5
Lamb La WHLY OX33 ......45 F2
Lambourn HI
Lambourn Rd COW/LTMR OX4 ..54 D1
Lambrick Wy ABGD OX14 ......63 E1
Lambs Cl KID OX5 ......10 A3
Lambton Cl COW/LTMR OX4 ..42 C2
Lammas Cl ABGD OX14 ......61 F2
Lancut Rd WITNEY OX28 ......20 D1
Landseer Wk ABGD OX14 ......60 A5
Lane Cl KID OX5 ......10 A3
The Lane STAD OX44 ......53 H2
Langdale Gv WITNEY OX28 ....20 B4
Langford La KID OX5 ......9 F3
Langford Locks KID OX5 ......9 F2
Langley Cl HEAD OX3 ......35 F4
Langley Rd ABGD OX14 ......55 H5
Lanham Wy COW/LTMR OX4 ..51 G1
Lansdowne Rd 54 C1
Larch End STAD OX44 ......53 H4
The Larches HEAD OX3 ......36 A3
Larch La RW/EYN OX29 ......21 H2
Larkfields HEAD OX3 ......42 A2
Lark Hill OXN/BOT/CM OX2 ..26 B1
Larkhill Pl ABGD OX14 ......60 D1
Larkhill Rd ABGD OX14 ......60 D2
Larkins La HEAD OX3 ......35 H3
Lashford La MCHM/KBPZ OX13 ..47 F5
Lathbury Rd OXN/BOT/CM OX2 .33 E1
Latimer Rd HEAD OX3 ......35 E4
Laurel Farm Cl HEAD OX3 ......36 A1
Lavender Vw RW/EYN OX29 ..21 H1
Lawrence La COW/LTMR OX4 ..42 A4
Lawrence Rd COW/LTMR OX4 ..42 A4
Leafield Rd COW/LTMR OX4 ..42 A3
Leckford Pl OXN/BOT/CM OX2 .33 F3

Leckford Rd OXN/BOT/CM OX2 .33 F3
Ledgers Cl COW/LTMR OX4 ..51 E2
Lee Av ABGD OX14 ......60 C5
Lee Cl KID OX5 ......9 H3
Leiden Rd HEAD OX3 ......42 C1
Leigh Cl RW/EYN OX29 ......12 B3
Leigh Cft MCHM/KBPZ OX13 ..47 G5
Lely Ct ABGD OX14 ......60 C5
Lenthall Rd ABGD OX14 ......60 C5
Leon Cl COW/LTMR OX4 ......41 F1
Leopold St COW/LTMR OX4 ..41 F2
Lesparre Cl ABGD OX14 ......62 B3
Letcombe Av ABGD OX14 ......60 C2
Levery Cl ABGD OX14 ......61 F2
Lewell Av HEAD OX3 ......42 A5
Lewin Cl COW/LTMR OX4 ......42 A5
Lewis Cl HEAD OX3 ......36 A4
Leyshon Rd WHLY OX33 ......45 E2
Leys Pl COW/LTMR OX4 ......41 G2
The Ley COW/LTMR OX4 ......5 E4
Liddell Rd COW/LTMR OX4 ..42 A5
Liddiard Cl OX/KTN OX1 ......50 A4
Lime Rd OXN/BOT/CM OX2 ..39 F2
Lime Wk HEAD OX3 ......42 C1
Lincoln Rd OX/KTN OX1 ......40 D4
Lincombe La OX/KTN OX1 ......48 C5
Lincraft Cl KID OX5 ......17 F2
Lindsay Dr ABGD OX14 ......56 B5
Linkside Av OX/KTN OX1 ......25 H1
Links Rd OX/KTN OX1 ......50 A4
The Link HEAD OX3 ......34 A2
Linnet Cl COW/LTMR OX4 ......51 H5
Linton Rd OXN/BOT/CM OX2 ..33 G1
Little Acreage HEAD OX3 ......27 F5
Little Blenheim KID OX5 ......16 C3
Little Brewery St
  COW/LTMR OX4 ......3 K4
Little Bury COW/LTMR OX4 ..52 A2
Little Clarendon St OX/KTN OX1 .2 C1
Littlegate OX/KTN OX1 ......2 D5
Littlegate St OX/KTN OX1 ......2 D5
Littlehay Rd COW/LTMR OX4 ..41 H4
Little Howe Cl ABGD OX14 ....57 E4
Littlemore Rd COW/LTMR OX4 .42 A5
Littleworth Pk WHLY OX33 ....44 B1
Littleworth Rd WHLY OX33 ....44 B1
Lobelia Rd COW/LTMR OX4 ..51 H2
Lock Crs KID OX5 ......17 G2
Lockheart Crs COW/LTMR OX4 .42 B5
Lockway ABGD OX14 ......61 F1
Loddon Cl ABGD OX14 ......61 F1
Lodge Cl HEAD OX3 ......27 F4
Lodge Rd RW/EYN OX29 ......7 F4
Logic La OX/KTN OX1 ......3 G4
Lombard St ABGD OX14 * 60 D4
London Pl COW/LTMR OX4 ......3 K4
London Rd HEAD OX3 ......36 A3
  WHLY OX33 ......44 D1
Long Cl HEAD OX3 ......42 C1
  OXN/BOT/CM OX2 ......38 D1
Longfellow Dr ABGD OX14 ....60 A5
Longfields MCHM/KBPZ OX13 .58 D3
Long Ford Cl OX/KTN OX1 ......2 D7
Long Furlong Rd
  MCHM/KBPZ OX13 ......55 F3
Long Gnd COW/LTMR OX4 ..51 G3
Longlands Rd COW/LTMR OX4 .51 F1
Long La COW/LTMR OX4 ......51 E1
Longmead ABGD OX14 ......60 C2
Long Tow MCHM/KBPZ OX13 .55 F5
Longwall St OX/KTN OX1 ......3 G3
Longworth Rd
  OXN/BOT/CM OX2 ......33 E3
Lonsdale Rd OXN/BOT/CM OX2 .26 D5
Lovelace Cl ABGD OX14 ......56 A4
Lovelace Dr KID OX5 ......10 C5
Lovelace Rd OXN/BOT/CM OX2 .26 A1
Lowell Pl WITNEY OX28 ......21 E5
Lower Farm La COW/LTMR OX4 .57 H1
Lower Fisher Rw OX/KTN OX1 ..2 C5
Lower Rd RW/EYN OX29 ......7 F5
Lower St KID OX5 ......11 H5
Loyd Cl ABGD OX14 ......56 A4
Lucca Dr ABGD OX14 ......62 D1
Lucerne Rd OXN/BOT/CM OX2 .26 C3
Lumberd Rd ABGD OX14 ......56 B5
Luther Ct OX/KTN OX1 ......2 E6
Luther St OX/KTN OX1 ......2 E6
Lydia Cl HEAD OX3 ......35 H2
Lye Va HEAD OX3 ......42 B2
Lyford Cl ABGD OX14 ......62 B5
Lyford Wy ABGD OX14 ......56 B5
Lyndworth Cl HEAD OX3 ......35 H3
Lyneham Cl WITNEY OX28 ....20 C2
Lyne Rd KID OX5 ......9 G4
Lynges Cl ABGD OX14 ......56 B5
Lynn Cl HEAD OX3 ......34 B2
Lynton La RW/EYN OX29 ......23 H1
Lyon Cl ABGD OX14 ......61 E1
Lytton Rd COW/LTMR OX4 ..41 G4

M

Maberley Cl ABGD OX14 ......60 A5
Magdalen Br OX/KTN OX1 ......3 H4
Magdalen Rd COW/LTMR OX4 .41 F2
Magdalen St OX/KTN OX1 ......2 D2
Magnette Cl ABGD OX14 ......60 D3
Magnolia Cl KID OX5 ......17 G1
Magpie La OX/KTN OX1 ......3 F3
Maidcroft Rd COW/LTMR OX4 ..42 A4
Maidley Cl WITNEY OX28 ......21 G1
Main Av COW/LTMR OX4 ......50 C5
Main Rd RW/EYN OX29 ......6 B4
Malford Rd HEAD OX3 ......35 H2
Mallard Cl COW/LTMR OX4 ..51 F2

Mallard Dr WITNEY OX28 ......21 E4
Maltfield Rd HEAD OX3 ......34 C1
Mandelbrote Dr COW/LTMR OX4 ..56 A5
Mandlebrote Dr
  COW/LTMR OX4 ......50 D3
  ABGD OX14 ......64 D5
  RW/EYN OX29 ......23 C1
Manor Cl ABGD OX14 ......60 C4
Manor Ct ABGD OX14 ......43 C3
Manor Farm Rd WHLY OX33 ..45 E3
Manor Gv OX/KTN OX1 ......50 A5
Manor Pl OX/KTN OX1 ......3 H2
Manor Rd MCHM/KBPZ OX13...47 C5
  OX/KTN OX1 ......3 H2
  WDSTK OX20 ......7 H4
  WITNEY OX28 ......21 G4
Manor Wy KID OX5 ......11 H4
Mansell Cl RW/EYN OX29 ......14 A2
Mansfield Rd OX/KTN OX1 ......3 F1
Manzil Wy COW/LTMR OX4 ..41 G1
Maple Av KID OX5 ......17 G1
Maple Cl OXN/BOT/CM OX2 ..39 F1
Marcham Rd ABGD OX14 ......62 A4
  MCHM/KBPZ OX13 ......59 E4
Margaret Rd HEAD OX3 ......35 F4
Marigold Cl COW/LTMR OX4 ..51 H5
Marina Wy ABGD OX14 ......63 F1
Marjoram Cl COW/LTMR OX4 ..51 H5
Market Pl ABGD OX14 ......60 D4
  WDSTK OX20 ......4 C5
Market Sq WITNEY OX28 ......21 F3
Market St OX/KTN OX1 ......2 E3
Mark Rd HEAD OX3 ......35 G5
Marlborough Av KID OX5 ......9 H5
Marlborough Cl COW/LTMR OX4 .50 D2
  RW/EYN OX29 ......23 C1
Marlborough Ct
  OXN/BOT/CM OX2 ......32 D5
Marlborough Crs RW/EYN OX29 ..6 A5
  WDSTK OX20 ......4 C5
Marlborough Dr ABGD OX14 ..63 E1
Marlborough La WITNEY OX28 .21 E3
Marlborough Pl RW/EYN OX29 .22 C3
Marlborough Rd OX/KTN OX1 ..2 D7
Marriott Cl OXN/BOT/CM OX2 ..26 B2
Marshall Rd COW/LTMR OX4 ..42 B5
Marsh Cl KID OX5 ......17 E5
Marsh La COW/LTMR OX4 ......34 C1
Marsh Rd COW/LTMR OX4 ......42 A3
Marston Ferry Rd 26 C5
Marston Rd HEAD OX3 ......34 B2
Marston St COW/LTMR OX4 ..3 K6
Mascall Av HEAD OX3 ......42 C2
Masefield Crs ABGD OX14 ......60 A5
Masey Cl HEAD OX3 ......35 F5
Masons Rd HEAD OX3 ......35 H2
Mather Rd HEAD OX3 ......35 H2
Mathews Wy MCHM/KBPZ OX13 .54 D1
Mattock Cl HEAD OX3 ......35 H4
Mattock Wy ABGD OX14 ......56 A5
Mavor Cl WDSTK OX20 ......4 D3
Mayfair Rd COW/LTMR OX4 ..41 H5
Mayfield Rd OXN/BOT/CM OX2 .30 B4
  OXN/BOT/CM OX2 ......33 E3
Mayott's Rd ABGD OX14 ......60 D4
Meaden HI HEAD OX3 ......34 D1
Meadow Cl RW/EYN OX29 ..30 B3
Meadow La COW/LTMR OX4 ..41 E2
Meadow Prospect
  OXN/BOT/CM OX2 ......25 F3
Meadowside ABGD OX14 ......60 C4
Meadow Vw KID OX5 ......10 A3
Meadow Vw Rd OX/KTN OX1 ..50 A4
Meadow Wy WDSTK OX20 ......5 E4
Meadow Wy KID OX5 ......16 D3
Mead Rd KID OX5 ......17 E4
Meads Cl ABGD OX14 ......60 A5
Mead Wy KID OX5 ......10 A5
Medlicott Dr ABGD OX14 ......55 H4
Medway Cl MCHM/KBPZ OX13 .55 E4
Medway Rd MCHM/KBPZ OX13 .55 E4
Meliebourne Cl COW/LTMR OX4 .51 H3
Mercury Rd COW/LTMR OX4 ..52 A2
Mere Rd OXN/BOT/CM OX2 ..26 A1
Merewood Av KID OX5 ......17 E5
Merlin Rd COW/LTMR OX4 ......51 C2
  MCHM/KBPZ OX13 ......55 E4
Merrivale Sq OXN/BOT/CM OX2 .33 E2
Merton Cl RW/EYN OX29 ......22 B4
Merton Gv OX/KTN OX1 ......3 G4
Merton St OX/KTN OX1 ......3 C4
Merton Wy KID OX5 ......16 D3
Metcalf Cl ABGD OX14 ......63 E1
Meyseys Rd HEAD OX3 ......42 C2
Mickle Wy WHLY OX33 ......37 E2
Middle Rd WHLY OX33 ......45 E4
Middle St KID OX5 ......11 H4
Middle Wy KID OX5 ......11 H4
  OXN/BOT/CM OX2 ......33 E2
Midget Cl ABGD OX14 ......60 B5
Mileway Gdns HEAD OX3 ......35 E5
Milkbank OXN/BOT/CM OX2 ..25 D3
Mill End KID OX5 ......10 C4
Miller Rd WHLY OX33 ......45 E2
Miller's Acre OXN/BOT/CM OX2 .26 B2
Millers Ms WITNEY OX28 ......21 F4
Mill La COW/LTMR OX4 ......41 F5
  HEAD OX3 ......27 E4
  RW/EYN OX29 ......22 D2
Millmoor Crs RW/EYN OX29 ..22 C3
Mill Paddock ABGD OX14 ......60 A5
Mill Rd KID OX5 ......58 D5
  OXN/BOT/CM OX2 ......25 F3
Mill St OXN/BOT/CM OX2 ......33 C6
  KID OX5 ......11 C5
  OXN/BOT/CM OX2 ......26 C5
  RW/EYN OX29 ......23 C1
  WHLY OX33 ......29 H4

WITNEY OX28 .....21 E2
Millway Cl OXN/BOT/CM OX2 .....25 H5
Millwood End RW/EYN OX29 .....8 A3
Millwood V RW/EYN OX29 .....6 A4
Milne Pl HEAD OX3 .....34 D2
Milton Crs WHLY OX33 .....37 F2
Milton Rd COW/LTMR OX4 .....41 H3
Minchery Rd COW/LTMR OX4 .....50 D2
Minchins Cl ABGD OX14 .....60 D2
Minster Rd COW/LTMR OX4 .....41 G1
Mirfield Rd WITNEY OX28 .....20 C3
Mistletoe Gn COW/LTMR OX4 .....51 G3
Mitchell Cl MCHM/KBPZ OX13 .....54 C1
Moberly Cl COW/LTMR OX4 .....3 K6
Mole Pl COW/LTMR OX4 .....51 H5
Monks Cl COW/LTMR OX4 .....51 F2
Monmouth Rd OX/KTN OX1 .....40 D4
Mons Wy ABGD OX14 .....60 B1
Montagu Rd COW/LTMR OX4 .....39 E1
Moody Rd HEAD OX3 .....34 B3
Moor Av WITNEY OX28 .....21 E2
Moorbank COW/LTMR OX4 .....51 G1
Moorland Cl WITNEY OX28 .....20 D2
Moorland Rd WITNEY OX28 .....20 D3
The Moorlands KID OX5 .....9 H3
The Moors KID OX5 .....9 H5
Moreton Rd OXN/BOT/CM OX2 .....33 G2
Morland Cl WHLY OX33 .....44 D1
Morland Rd MCHM/KBPZ OX13 .....58 D4
Morrell Av COW/LTMR OX4 .....41 F1
Morrell Cl KID OX5 .....9 H5
Morrell Crs COW/LTMR OX4 .....50 C2
Morris Crs COW/LTMR OX4 .....41 H5
Mortimer Dr HEAD OX3 .....34 A2
Mortimer Rd COW/LTMR OX4 .....50 B1
Morton Av KID OX5 .....17 G1
Morton Cl KID OX5 .....61 G2
  KID OX5 .....10 A5
The Motte ABGD OX14 .....60 D2
Mountfield Rd WITNEY OX28 .....20 C4
Mount Pl OXN/BOT/CM OX2 * 2 A1
Mount St OXN/BOT/CM OX2 .....2 A1
Mulberry Dr WHLY OX33 .....44 D1
Mulcaster Av KID OX5 .....10 B5
Mullard Wy ABGD OX14 .....60 C5
Museum Rd OX/KTN OX1 .....2 E1
Musson Cl ABGD OX14 .....60 C4
Myrtle Cl RW/EYN OX29 .....6 B4

N

Napier Ct ABGD OX14 .....61 F3
Napier Rd COW/LTMR OX4 .....42 B5
Nash Dr ABGD OX14 .....60 A4
Nash La RW/EYN OX29 .....13 G1
Navigation Wy
  OXN/BOT/CM OX2 .....33 E2
Nelson St OXN/BOT/CM OX2 .....2 B2
Nene Rd MCHM/KBPZ OX13 .....58 C5
Nether Durnford Cl HEAD OX3 .....42 C2
Netherwoods Rd HEAD OX3 .....35 H4
Nettlebed Md COW/LTMR OX4 .....41 G3
New College La OX/KTN OX1 .....3 F5
New Cross Rd HEAD OX3 .....35 G3
New High St HEAD OX3 .....35 F4
New Inn Hall St OX/KTN OX1 .....2 D4
New Inn Rd HEAD OX3 .....29 E1
Newland WITNEY OX28 .....21 C2
Newland Ml WITNEY OX28 .....21 G3
Newland St RW/EYN OX29 .....22 C3
Newlin Cl COW/LTMR OX4 .....50 B1
Newman La ABGD OX14 .....62 B3
Newman Rd COW/LTMR OX4 .....50 D1
Newmill La RW/EYN OX29 .....20 C1
Newport Cl KID OX5 .....17 F1
Newport Rd ABGD OX14 .....57 E4
  MCHM/KBPZ OX13 .....58 C4
  OX/KTN OX1 .....2 C4
  RW/EYN OX29 .....6 B4
  WDSTK OX20 .....4 D4
New St ABGD OX14 .....60 D5
Newton Rd OX/KTN OX1 .....40 D2
New Yatt Rd WITNEY OX28 .....21 G1
Nicholas Av HEAD OX3 .....34 B2
Nicholson Rd HEAD OX3 .....34 B3
Nightingale Av COW/LTMR OX4 .....51 H3
Nixon Rd COW/LTMR OX4 .....41 F4
Nobles Cl OXN/BOT/CM OX2 .....33 E1
Nobles La OXN/BOT/CM OX2 .....38 C1
Norbrook Cl ABGD OX14 .....56 C5
Norfolk Cl COW/LTMR OX4 .....56 D5
Norfolk St OX/KTN OX1 .....2 D5
Norham Gdns
  OXN/BOT/CM OX2 .....33 G3
Norman Rd OXN/BOT/CM OX2 .....33 G2
Norman Av ABGD OX14 .....61 E1
Normandy Crs COW/LTMR OX4 .....42 C4
Norman Smith Rd
  COW/LTMR OX4 .....51 H5
Norreys Av OX/KTN OX1 .....40 D3
Norreys Rd OXN/BOT/CM OX2 .....38 B4
Norris Cl ABGD OX14 .....56 B5
Northampton Rd OX/KTN OX1 .....40 D4
North Av ABGD OX14 .....56 A5
Northcourt La ABGD OX14 .....61 E1
Northcourt Rd ABGD OX14 .....60 D1
Northcourt Wk ABGD OX14 .....61 E1
Northern By-Pass Rd HEAD OX3 .....54 D1
  OXN/BOT/CM OX2 .....25 F1
Northfield Rd ABGD OX14 .....56 A4
  HEAD OX3 .....35 G2
North Hinksey La
  OXN/BOT/CM OX2 .....39 G1
Northmoor Rd
  OXN/BOT/CM OX2 .....33 G3
North Parade Av
  OXN/BOT/CM OX2 .....33 F2
North Pl HEAD OX3 .....35 F3

North Quay ABGD OX14 .....63 F1
North St KID OX5 .....11 H4
  MCHM/KBPZ OX13 .....58 C3
  OXN/BOT/CM OX2 .....33 F5
North Wy HEAD OX3 .....35 G2
  OXN/BOT/CM OX2 .....26 A2
Northwood Rd RW/EYN OX29 .....20 A2
Norton Cl HEAD OX3 .....35 F4
Norwell Rd COW/LTMR OX4 .....50 C1
Nuffield Rd HEAD OX3 .....42 C1
Nuffield Wy ABGD OX14 .....60 A3
Nuneham Sq ABGD OX14 .....60 C2
Nunnery Cl COW/LTMR OX4 .....51 F2
Nurseries Rd KID OX5 .....9 H5
Nursery Cl HEAD OX3 .....35 E4
Nursery Rd RW/EYN OX29 .....12 C1
The Nursery ABGD OX14 .....63 C5
Nuthatch Cl COW/LTMR OX4 .....51 G3
Nyatt Rd ABGD OX14 .....61 G2
Nye Bevan Cl COW/LTMR OX4 .....41 G1

O

Oak Av ABGD OX14 .....57 E1
Oak Dr KID OX5 .....10 B5
Oakes La OXN/BOT/CM OX2 .....30 C4
Oakland Cl RW/EYN OX29 .....13 F1
Oakmead RW/EYN OX29 .....21 H1
Oak Mill Cl ABGD OX14 .....60 B4
Oakthorpe Pl OXN/BOT/CM OX2 .....26 B5
Oakthorpe Rd
  OXN/BOT/CM OX2 .....26 B5
Oatlands Rd OXN/BOT/CM OX2 .....32 D5
Observatory St
  OXN/BOT/CM OX2 .....33 F3
Ock St ABGD OX14 .....60 C4
Old Barn Gnd HEAD OX3 .....42 D2
Old Chapel Cl KID OX5 .....10 A4
Old Farm Cl ABGD OX14 .....61 G2
Old Greyfriars St OX/KTN OX1 .....2 D5
Old High St HEAD OX3 .....35 F4
Old London Rd WHLY OX33 .....45 E1
Old Marston Rd HEAD OX3 .....34 B2
Old Nursery Vw OX/KTN OX1 .....49 H2
The Old Pound
  MCHM/KBPZ OX13 .....54 D2
Old Rd HEAD OX3 .....35 H5
  WHLY OX33 .....45 H1
Old School COW/LTMR OX4 .....42 A3
Old Station Yd ABGD OX14 .....60 D3
Old Witney Rd RW/EYN OX29 .....22 C2
Oliver Rd COW/LTMR OX4 .....42 C4
Orchard Cl ABGD OX14 .....61 E1
  RW/EYN OX29 .....6 A3
  RW/EYN OX29 .....23 C1
  WHLY OX33 .....44 D2
Orchard Ct COW/LTMR OX4 .....41 H5
Orchard Field La WDSTK OX20 .....8 B1
Orchard La OX/KTN OX1 .....48 A3
Orchard Rd OXN/BOT/CM OX2 .....38 C1
The Orchard RW/EYN OX29 .....22 D4
Orchard Wy COW/LTMR OX4 .....51 E1
  KID OX5 .....10 B5
  MCHM/KBPZ OX13 .....58 D4
  WITNEY OX28 .....21 E3
Oriel St OX/KTN OX1 .....3 F4
Orkney Pl WITNEY OX28 .....20 D3
Orpwood Wy ABGD OX14 .....60 A4
Osberton Rd OXN/BOT/CM OX2 .....26 A4
Osborne Cl KID OX5 .....17 F1
  OXN/BOT/CM OX2 .....25 H3
Osler Rd HEAD OX3 .....35 E3
Osney La OX/KTN OX1 .....2 B4
Osney Md OXN/BOT/CM OX2 .....2 A6
Oswestry Rd COW/LTMR OX4 .....40 D4
Otters Reach OX/KTN OX1 .....50 A3
Otwell Cl ABGD OX14 .....56 B5
Ouseley Cl HEAD OX3 .....34 B2
Outram Rd COW/LTMR OX4 .....41 H4
The Oval COW/LTMR OX4 .....50 C1
Overbrooke Gdns
  COW/LTMR OX4 .....52 A2
Overdale Cl HEAD OX3 .....35 C2
Owlington Cl OXN/BOT/CM OX2 .....32 A5
Oxeye Ct COW/LTMR OX4 .....51 C4
Oxford Canal Wk KID OX5 .....17 F5
Oxford Cl OXN/BOT/CM OX2 .....33 E1
Oxford Hl WITNEY OX28 .....21 H3
Oxford Rd ABGD OX14 .....61 E2
  COW/LTMR OX4 .....52 B4
  HEAD OX3 .....34 B1
  KID OX5 .....10 A5
  OXN/BOT/CM OX2 .....38 B4
  RW/EYN OX29 .....23 C5
  STAD OX44 .....52 B1
  WDSTK OX20 .....5 E4
  WHLY OX33 .....45 F4
Oxford St WDSTK OX20 .....4 D4
Oxlease WITNEY OX28 .....21 H4
Oxpens Rd OX/KTN OX1 .....2 B4

P

Packhorse La
  MCHM/KBPZ OX13 .....58 D4
The Paddock OX/KTN OX1 .....50 A5
The Paddocks KID OX5 .....16 D3
Paddox Cl OXN/BOT/CM OX2 .....26 A3
Paget Rd COW/LTMR OX4 .....42 C5
Pagisters Rd ABGD OX14 .....56 C5
Painswick Cl WITNEY OX28 .....20 C2
Palmer Rd ABGD OX14 .....60 C5
Palmer Rd HEAD OX3 .....35 G5
Paradise Sq OX/KTN OX1 .....2 C5

Paradise St OX/KTN OX1 .....2 C4
Park Av OX5 .....9 H3
Park Cl KID OX5 .....16 D4
  OXN/BOT/CM OX2 .....26 A5
  RW/EYN OX29 .....12 C2
  WDSTK OX20 .....7 H2
Park Crs ABGD OX14 .....60 B3
Park End Pl OX/KTN OX1 .....2 B4
Park End St OX/KTN OX1 .....2 B4
Parker St COW/LTMR OX4 .....41 H5
Park Hl WHLY OX33 .....37 C5
Parklands RW/EYN OX29 .....13 F1
Park La MCHM/KBPZ OX13 .....46 A5
  RW/EYN OX29 .....6 D3
  WDSTK OX20 .....7 H3
Park Rd ABGD OX14 .....60 C3
  RW/EYN OX29 .....12 B2
  WITNEY OX28 .....20 D2
Park Side MCHM/KBPZ OX13 .....58 C4
  WDSTK OX20 .....7 H3
Parkside RW/EYN OX29 .....12 C2
  WITNEY OX28 .....21 F5
Parks Rd OX/KTN OX1 .....3 F3
Park St WDSTK OX20 .....7 H3
The Park OXN/BOT/CM OX2 .....38 A4
Park Town OXN/BOT/CM OX2 .....33 G2
Park Wy HEAD OX3 .....27 F4
Parry Cl HEAD OX3 .....34 B5
Parsons Md ABGD OX14 .....60 C1
Parsons Pl COW/LTMR OX4 .....41 G1
Partridge Pl KID OX5 .....9 G4
Partridge Wk COW/LTMR OX4 .....52 A3
Pattison Pl COW/LTMR OX4 .....50 C1
Pauling Rd HEAD OX3 .....35 G5
Peachcroft Rd ABGD OX14 .....56 C5
Peacock Rd HEAD OX3 .....34 B5
Peartree Cl COW/LTMR OX4 .....51 H5
Peat Moors HEAD OX3 .....42 B1
Peel Pl OX/KTN OX1 .....40 D4
Peep-o-day La ABGD OX14 .....61 G3
Pegasus Ct OX/KTN OX1 * 2 E7
Pegasus Rd COW/LTMR OX4 .....51 H1
Pelican Pl RW/EYN OX29 .....22 C3
Pembroke Sq OX/KTN OX1 * 2 E5
Pembroke St OX/KTN OX1 .....2 E4
Pen La ABGD OX14 .....60 D5
Penn Cl ABGD OX14 .....56 C5
Pennycress Rd COW/LTMR OX4 .....52 A2
Penny Farthing Pl OX/KTN OX1 .....2 D4
Pennywell Dr OXN/BOT/CM OX2 .....26 B1
Penslose WITNEY OX28 .....21 C2
Penson's Gdns COW/LTMR OX4 * 3 J4
Peppercorn Av HEAD OX3 .....42 C1
Percy St COW/LTMR OX4 .....41 F3
Peregrine Rd COW/LTMR OX4 .....51 H2
Periwinkle Pl COW/LTMR OX4 .....51 H2
Perkins OX/KTN OX1 .....49 H2
Perrin St HEAD OX3 .....35 E4
Perrott Cl RW/EYN OX29 .....12 A1
Peterley Rd COW/LTMR OX4 .....42 D3
Peter's Wy COW/LTMR OX4 .....51 E2
Pether Rd HEAD OX3 .....35 G5
Petre Pl KID OX5 .....10 B4
Pettiwell STAD OX44 .....52 D4
Pheasant Wk COW/LTMR OX4 .....52 A3
Phelps Pl COW/LTMR OX4 .....3 K4
The Phelps KID OX5 .....9 H5
Phipps Rd COW/LTMR OX4 .....42 B5
Phoebe Ct OXN/BOT/CM OX2 .....26 A5
Pickett Av HEAD OX3 .....42 C2
Picklers Hill ABGD OX14 .....56 C5
Pigeon House La RW/EYN OX29 .....13 H2
Pike Ter OX/KTN OX1 .....2 D5
Pimpernel Cl COW/LTMR OX4 .....52 A2
Pine Cl COW/LTMR OX4 .....52 A1
Pine Ri RW/EYN OX29 .....21 H1
Pinkhill La RW/EYN OX29 .....22 C5
Pinnocks Wy OXN/BOT/CM OX2 .....38 D1
Pinsley Rd RW/EYN OX29 .....6 B5
Piper St HEAD OX3 .....35 F4
Pipit Cl COW/LTMR OX4 .....51 G3
Pipkin Wy COW/LTMR OX4 .....41 G3
Pipley Furlong COW/LTMR OX4 .....50 D2
Pitts Rd HEAD OX3 .....35 G3
Pixey Pl OXN/BOT/CM OX2 .....25 H3
The Plain OX/KTN OX1 .....3 H4
Plane Tree Wy WDSTK OX20 .....5 E4
Plantation Rd
  OXN/BOT/CM OX2 .....33 F3
Plater Dr OXN/BOT/CM OX2 .....33 E2
Playfield Rd OX/KTN OX1 .....50 A5
Ploughley Cl KID OX5 .....9 H5
Pochard Pl COW/LTMR OX4 .....51 H3
Polecat End La WHLY OX33 .....37 F2
Polstead Rd OXN/BOT/CM OX2 .....33 F2
Pond Cl HEAD OX3 .....35 A3
Ponds La HEAD OX3 .....27 F5
Pony Rd COW/LTMR OX4 .....42 D3
Pope's Piece WITNEY OX28 .....20 D2
Poplar Cl KID OX5 .....17 H1
  OX5 .....9 G3
Poplar Gv OX/KTN OX1 .....50 A4
Poplar Rd OXN/BOT/CM OX2 .....32 A5
Portland Rd OXN/BOT/CM OX2 .....33 F2
Potenger Wy ABGD OX14 .....60 B4
Pottery Piece COW/LTMR OX4 .....51 G3
Pottle Cl OXN/BOT/CM OX2 .....25 H3
Poulton Pl COW/LTMR OX4 .....51 H5
Pound Cl KID OX5 .....16 D3
Pound Field Cl HEAD OX3 .....35 G1
Pound La RW/EYN OX29 .....23 C4
  WHLY OX33 .....29 C4
Powell Cl WHLY OX33 .....37 F2
Preachers La OX/KTN OX1 .....2 C5
Preston Rd ABGD OX14 .....60 B5
Prestwich Pl OXN/BOT/CM OX2 .....32 D5
Prichard Rd HEAD OX3 .....34 C3
Primrose Pl COW/LTMR OX4 .....51 H3
Prince Gv ABGD OX14 .....56 A4
Princes Ride WDSTK OX20 .....5 E4
Princes St COW/LTMR OX4 .....41 F1
Prior's Forge OXN/BOT/CM OX2 .....26 B2
Priory La MCHM/KBPZ OX13 .....58 D4
Priory Rd COW/LTMR OX4 .....51 E2

Puck La WITNEY OX28 .....21 F2
Pudsey Cl ABGD OX14 .....63 E1
Pulker Cl COW/LTMR OX4 .....42 A5
Pullens Fld HEAD OX3 .....34 C4
Pullens La HEAD OX3 .....34 C4
Purcell Rd HEAD OX3 .....34 B5
Purslane ABGD OX14 .....61 F2
Pusey La OX/KTN OX1 .....2 D3
Pusey Pl OX/KTN OX1 * 2 D3
Pusey St OX/KTN OX1 .....2 D2
Pykes Cl ABGD OX14 .....56 B5
Pytenry Cl ABGD OX14 .....56 B4

Q

The Quadrant ABGD OX14 .....61 F3
Quarry End KID OX5 .....9 H5
Quarry High St HEAD OX3 .....35 C5
Quarry Hollow HEAD OX3 .....35 C4
Quarry Rd HEAD OX3 .....35 C4
  MCHM/KBPZ OX13 .....49 E5
  WITNEY OX28 .....21 E1
Quarry School Pl HEAD OX3 .....35 C4
Quartermain Cl COW/LTMR OX4 .....41 H3
Queen Emmas Dyke
  WITNEY OX28 .....20 D3
Queens Av KID OX5 .....10 C5
Queens Cl OXN/BOT/CM OX2 .....38 D1
Queens La OX/KTN OX1 .....3 F5
  OX/KTN OX1 .....22 C4
Queen St ABGD OX14 .....60 D5
  OX/KTN OX1 .....2 D4
  RW/EYN OX29 .....22 C4

R

Rackham Pl OXN/BOT/CM OX2 .....26 A5
Radcliffe Rd COW/LTMR OX4 .....41 F4
Radcliffe Sq OX/KTN OX1 .....3 F3
Radford Cl COW/LTMR OX4 .....50 B1
Radley Rd ABGD OX14 .....61 E2
Rahere Rd COW/LTMR OX4 .....51 E1
Railway La COW/LTMR OX4 .....50 C2
Rainbow Wy ABGD OX14 .....56 B4
Raleigh Crs WITNEY OX28 .....20 B3
Raleigh Park Rd
  OXN/BOT/CM OX2 .....39 G2
Rampion Cl OXN/BOT/CM OX2 .....52 A2
Ramsey Rd HEAD OX3 .....35 C5
Ramsons Wy ABGD OX14 .....61 F2
Randolph St COW/LTMR OX4 .....41 F2
Range Rd RW/EYN OX29 .....20 A3
Rawlings Gv ABGD OX14 .....60 B2
Rawlinson Rd
  OXN/BOT/CM OX2 .....33 F1
Rawson Cl OXN/BOT/CM OX2 .....25 H2
Raymund Rd HEAD OX3 .....34 B1
Reade Av ABGD OX14 .....61 F2
Recreation Rd ABGD OX14 .....5 E4
Rectory La WDSTK OX20 .....7 H3
Rectory Rd COW/LTMR OX4 .....3 K5
Red Bridge Hollow OX/KTN OX1 .....40 C5
Red Copse La OX/KTN OX1 .....49 E2
Rede Cl HEAD OX3 .....42 C1
Redland Rd HEAD OX3 .....34 D1
Red Lion Sq OX/KTN OX1 * 2 D5
Redmoor Cl COW/LTMR OX4 .....51 E2
Redwood Cl COW/LTMR OX4 .....52 A2
Reedmace Cl COW/LTMR OX4 .....52 A2
Regent St COW/LTMR OX4 .....3 K7
Rest Harrow COW/LTMR OX4 .....51 H2
Rewley Rd OXN/BOT/CM OX2 .....2 B3
Reynolds Wy ABGD OX14 .....60 D1
Richards La OXN/BOT/CM OX2 .....26 A4
Richards Wy HEAD OX3 .....35 H4
Richmond Rd OXN/BOT/CM OX2 .....2 B2
Rickyard Cl OXN/BOT/CM OX2 .....26 A2
Riddell Pl OXN/BOT/CM OX2 .....26 A2
Ridgefield Rd COW/LTMR OX4 .....41 G2
Ridgemont Cl
  OXN/BOT/CM OX2 .....26 A4
Ridgeway OX/KTN OX1 .....48 B3
Ridgeway Rd HEAD OX3 .....35 H3
The Ridings HEAD OX3 .....42 D1
  KID OX5 .....9 H5
Ridley Rd COW/LTMR OX4 .....42 C5
Riely Cl RW/EYN OX29 .....6 C4
Riley Cl ABGD OX14 .....60 B4
Rimmer Cl HEAD OX3 .....34 B1
Ringwood Rd HEAD OX3 .....36 A3
Rippington Cl ABGD OX14 .....56 B5
Rippington Dr HEAD OX3 .....34 B2
The Rise HEAD OX3 .....11 C4
Rissington Dr WITNEY OX28 .....20 B4
River Cl ABGD OX14 .....60 C5
Rivermead Rd COW/LTMR OX4 .....50 B1
Riverside Gdns WITNEY OX28 .....21 F2
Riverside Rd OXN/BOT/CM OX2 .....33 E4
River Vw OX/KTN OX1 .....50 A3
Rivy Cl ABGD OX14 .....61 G2
Robert Robinson Av
  COW/LTMR OX4 .....51 E3
Robin Hl RW/EYN OX29 .....6 C4
Robsart Pl OXN/BOT/CM OX2 .....38 A5
Rock Edge HEAD OX3 .....35 F5
Rock Farm La COW/LTMR OX4 .....50 D4
Roger Dudman Wy
  OXN/BOT/CM OX2 .....2 A2
Rogers St OXN/BOT/CM OX2 .....26 B4
Rolfe Pl HEAD OX3 .....34 B5
Roman Rd WHLY OX33 .....45 E2
Roman Wy COW/LTMR OX4 .....42 D4
Rookery Cl MCHM/KBPZ OX13 .....59 H1

The Rookery KID OX5 .....9 H5
Roosevelt Dr HEAD OX3 .....34 A4
Roosevelt Rd RW/EYN OX29 .....20 C3
Rosamund Dr WDSTK OX20 .....20 A1
Rosamund Rd
  OXN/BOT/CM OX2
Rose Av ABGD OX14
Rose Gdns OXN/BOT/CM OX2
Rose Hl COW/LTMR OX4
Rose La OX/KTN OX1
Rose Pl OX/KTN OX1
Ross Ct OX/KTN OX1 *
Rotha Field Rd
  OXN/BOT/CM OX2
Roundham Cl KID OX5
The Roundway HEAD OX3
Routh Rd HEAD OX3
Rowan Cl KID OX5
Rowan Gv COW/LTMR OX4
Rowel Dr KID OX5
Rowland Cl OXN/BOT/CM OX2
Rowles Cl OX/KTN OX1
Rowney Pl COW/LTMR OX4
Rupert Rd COW/LTMR OX4
Rushmead Copse ABGD OX14
Ruskin Av COW/LTMR OX4
Russell Ct OXN/BOT/CM OX2
Russell St OXN/BOT/CM OX2
Rutherford Cl ABGD OX14
Rutherway OXN/BOT/CM OX2
Rutten La KID OX5
Rutters Cl KID OX5
Ryder Cl KID OX5
  OXN/BOT/CM OX2
Rymers La COW/LTMR OX4

S

Sadliers Ct ABGD OX14
Sadliers Cft STAD OX44
Sadler Wk OX/KTN OX1
Saffron Ct ABGD OX14
Sage Wk COW/LTMR OX4
St Aldate's OX/KTN OX1
St Amand Dr ABGD OX14
St Andrew's La HEAD OX3
St Andrew's Rd HEAD OX3
St Anne's Rd HEAD OX3
St Barnabas St
  OXN/BOT/CM OX2
St Bernard's Rd
  OXN/BOT/CM OX2
St Christopher's Pl
  COW/LTMR OX4
St Clement's St COW/LTMR OX4
St Cross Rd OX/KTN OX1
St Ebbes St OX/KTN OX1
St Edmund's La ABGD OX14 *
St Edward's Av
  OXN/BOT/CM OX2
St Georges Pl OX/KTN OX1 *
St Giles' OX/KTN OX1
St Helen's Ct ABGD OX14
St Helen's Ms ABGD OX14 *
St Helen's Ml ABGD OX14
St Helen's Wk ABGD OX14
St Helen's Whf ABGD OX14
St James Rd ABGD OX14
St John St OX/KTN OX1
St Johns Dr KID OX5
St John's Rd ABGD OX14
St Lawrence Rd OX/KTN OX1
St Leonard's Rd HEAD OX3
St Luke's Rd COW/LTMR OX4
St Margaret's Rd
  OXN/BOT/CM OX2
St Martin's Rd COW/LTMR OX4
St Mary's Cl COW/LTMR OX4
  KID OX5
  WHLY OX33
St Mary's Gn ABGD OX14
St Marys Md WITNEY OX28
St Mary's Rd COW/LTMR OX4
St Michael's Av ABGD OX14
St Michael's St OX/KTN OX1
St Nicholas Rd ABGD OX14 *
St Nicholas' Gn ABGD OX14
St Nicholas Rd COW/LTMR OX4
St Omer Rd COW/LTMR OX4
St Paul's Crs OXN/BOT/CM OX2
St Peter's Cl MCHM/KBPZ OX13
  RW/EYN OX29
St Peter's Rd ABGD OX14
  OXN/BOT/CM OX2
St Swithun's Rd OX/KTN OX1
St Thomas' St OX/KTN OX1
Salegate La COW/LTMR OX4
Salesian Gdns COW/LTMR OX4
Salford Rd HEAD OX3
Salisbury Crs OXN/BOT/CM OX2
Salter Cl OX/KTN OX1
Samphire Rd COW/LTMR OX4
Sandfield Rd HEAD OX3
Sandford Cl ABGD OX14
Sandford La OX/KTN OX1
Sandford Rd COW/LTMR OX4
Sandhill Rd KID OX5
Sand La HEAD OX3
Sandleigh Rd
  MCHM/KBPZ OX13
Sandy La COW/LTMR OX4
  OX/KTN OX1
Sandy La West COW/LTMR OX4
Saunders Rd COW/LTMR OX4
Savile Rd OX/KTN OX1

Rd COW/LTMR OX4 51 G1
ge Sq COW/LTMR OX4 * 51 G3
Wy HEAD OX3 34 D1
VEY OX28 21 E4
Rd ABGD OX14 60 B5
r Pl OXN/BOT/CM OX2 39 E2
iau Cl ABGD OX14 62 D1
Ct OXN/BOT/CM OX2 2 B1
La ABGD OX14 64 D5
Pl OX/KTN OX1 40 C3
Rd KID OX5 10 A4
Cl KID OX5 9 H5
Rd OXN/BOT/CM OX2 26 B3
urt Rd OXN/BOT/CM OX2 32 A5
Rd HEAD OX3 35 G3
od Rd ABGD OX14 60 D1
n Crs ABGD OX14 57 E5
n Cl HEAD OX3 35 H4
Rd MCHM/KBPZ OX13 55 F5
Cl ABGD OX14 61 G1
sbury Rd HEAD OX3 35 G1
speare Rd
/EYN OX29 22 B3
s Copse ABGD OX14 57 F5
stead Rd
HM/KBPZ OX13 58 C2
way Ct COW/LTMR OX4 41 G5
n Wy COW/LTMR OX4 51 E1
rd Pl HEAD OX3 35 F5
Cl ABGD OX14 61 E1
D OX3 35 H4
Rd COW/LTMR OX4 41 H3
erd Gdns ABGD OX14 60 A4
erds Hl COW/LTMR OX4 51 H3
ourne Rd WITNEY OX28 20 B3
f's Dr OXN/BOT/CM OX2 25 H3
ood Av ABGD OX14 61 E3
t OX/KTN OX1 2 E3
n Rd WDSTK OX20 5 F4
Lake Cl OX/KTN OX1 2 E6
Pl OXN/BOT/CM OX2 33 F3
La OX/KTN OX1 2 D4
e Cl HEAD OX3 42 C2
ver Kilns HEAD OX3 35 H5
es Cl ABGD OX14 56 B4
St COW/LTMR OX4 41 F2
le Cl COW/LTMR OX4 42 B4
Rd COW/LTMR OX4 41 G2
's Cl WHLY OX33 44 C1
ons Wy OX/KTN OX1 50 A4
iklaas Cl ABGD OX14 62 D1
Cl HEAD OX3 35 F5
ade HEAD OX3 42 C1
rs Ct RW/EYN OX29 6 A4
aker Cl HEAD OX3 35 H4
don Mede HEAD OX3 34 C2
shill Dr WITNEY OX28 20 B3
ers Cl OXN/BOT/CM OX2 38 D2
Rd COW/LTMR OX4 51 H1
Av ABGD OX14 55 H5
OX5 17 G2
by Cl MCHM/KBPZ OX13 46 A4
Cl KID OX5 17 H3
croft HEAD OX3 27 F5
dale Rd OXN/BOT/CM OX2 26 B3
end STAD OX44 53 E3
ern By-Pass Rd
/KTN OX1 40 A3
N/BOT/CM OX2 39 F1
field Rd COW/LTMR OX4 41 G1
lawn WITNEY OX28 20 D4
moor Pl
N/BOT/CM OX2 33 E2
moor Rd
N/BOT/CM OX2 33 E3
moor Wy ABGD OX14 60 C2
Pde OXN/BOT/CM OX2 26 A5
Parks Rd OX/KTN OX1 3 F1
n Quay ABGD OX14 63 F1
St OXN/BOT/CM OX2 40 A1
wood Rd RW/EYN OX29 20 A2
acre La RW/EYN OX29 22 B3
ey Pl OXN/BOT/CM OX2 26 B2
pears KID OX5 16 D2
dwell St OX/KTN OX1 2 D5
cer Av KID OX5 16 D3
cer Crs COW/LTMR OX4 41 G5
ove Cl ABGD OX14 55 H5
Rd MCHM/KBPZ OX13 55 E4
leberry Cl COW/LTMR OX4 51 G2
lers KID OX5 10 B4
ey Fld COW/LTMR OX4 51 G3
eys Cl ABGD OX14 57 F4
spinney ABGD OX14 60 B1
ner Cl HEAD OX3 35 G3
g Copse OX/KTN OX1 49 G1
gfield Dr ABGD OX14 60 C2
gfield Ov WITNEY OX28 20 D1
gfield Pk WITNEY OX28 20 D2
gfield Rd KID OX5 10 B5
XN/BOT/CM OX2 39 E1
g Gdns ABGD OX14 60 B3
g Hill Rd KID OX5 8 D5
g La COW/LTMR OX4 51 F2
EAD OX3 35 H3
HLY OX33 43 G2
g Rd ABGD OX14 60 B3
Springs WITNEY OX28 21 E4
ce Gdns COW/LTMR OX4 51 G4
ce Rd KID OX5 17 G1
Square ABGD OX14 60 D3
tchey La OXN/BOT/CM OX2 26 A3
e Cl OXN/BOT/CM OX2 2 B3
er Pl HEAD OX3 34 B2
field Rd HEAD OX3 34 D1
ford Dr ABGD OX14 60 D3
ley Cl KID OX5 16 D1
XN/BOT/CM OX2 39 F1
ley Rd COW/LTMR OX4 41 F2
sfeld Pl HEAD OX3 35 G5
sfield Cl HEAD OX3 35 H5
ton Cl WITNEY OX28 20 C3
ton Harcourt Rd
ITNEY OX28 21 H4
Stanton Rd OXN/BOT/CM OX2 39 G3
WHLY OX33 37 E1
Stanville Rd OXN/BOT/CM OX2 38 D2
Stanway Cl WITNEY OX28 20 B2
Stanway Rd HEAD OX3 35 H3
Stapleton Rd HEAD OX3 35 E4
Station Ap KID OX5 9 G3
Station La WITNEY OX28 21 E5
Station Rd ABGD OX14 60 D3
ABGD OX14 64 D2
RW/EYN OX29 22 C4
WHLY OX33 44 C1
Staunton Rd HEAD OX3 34 D3
Staverton Rd OXN/BOT/CM OX2 33 F1
Steep Ri HEAD OX3 35 E1
Stenton Cl ABGD OX14 60 C5
Stephen Rd HEAD OX3 35 E3
Sterling Cl KID OX5 10 A5
Sterling Rd KID OX5 10 A5
Sterling Road Ap KID OX5 10 A4
Stert St ABGD OX14 60 D3
Stevens Cl OXN/BOT/CM OX2 33 F2
Stevenson Dr ABGD OX14 60 B2
Steventon Rd ABGD OX14 62 B5
Stewart St OX/KTN OX1 40 C3
Stile Rd HEAD OX3 35 F3
Stimpsons Cl OXN/BOT/CM OX2 31 G5
Stockey End ABGD OX14 56 C5
Stockleys Rd HEAD OX3 34 C1
Stockmore St COW/LTMR OX4 3 J6
Stocks Tree Cl KID OX5 16 D3
Stoke Pl HEAD OX3 35 E2
Stone Cl OXN/BOT/CM OX2 31 H5
Stonehill La ABGD OX14 62 C1
Stonehill Wk ABGD OX14 62 D1
Stone Quarry La
COW/LTMR OX4 41 G5
Stone St COW/LTMR OX4 41 G1
Stonhouse Crs ABGD OX14 57 E5
Stonor Pl HEAD OX3 34 D4
Stoutsfield Cl KID OX5 16 C3
Stow Av WITNEY OX28 20 B3
Stowford Rd HEAD OX3 35 H2
Stowood Cl HEAD OX3 35 H5
Stratfield Rd KID OX5 17 G2
OXN/BOT/CM OX2 26 B4
Stratford Dr RW/EYN OX29 22 B3
Stratford St COW/LTMR OX4 3 J7
Stratton Wy ABGD OX14 60 D3
Stubble Cl OXN/BOT/CM OX2 38 C1
Stubbs Av HEAD OX3 42 C2
Sturges Cl HEAD OX3 35 F2
Suffolk Wy ABGD OX14 60 B4
Sugworth Crs ABGD OX14 57 E1
Sugworth La MCHM/KBPZ OX13 56 B1
Summerfield OX/KTN OX1 40 D3
Summer Flds ABGD OX14 56 B4
Summerhill Rd
OXN/BOT/CM OX2 26 B4
Summertown Ct
OXN/BOT/CM OX2 26 A4
Sunderland Av
OXN/BOT/CM OX2 25 H2
Sundew Cl COW/LTMR OX4 52 A2
Sunningwell Rd
MCHM/KBPZ OX13 55 G3
OX/KTN OX1 40 D4
Sunny Ri WHLY OX33 43 H3
Sunnyside COW/LTMR OX4 42 B3
WHLY OX33 45 E1
Sutton Cl ABGD OX14 60 D3
Sutton Rd HEAD OX3 34 D1
Sutton Wick La ABGD OX14 62 B3
Swain Ct WITNEY OX28 * 21 F5
Swallow Cl COW/LTMR OX4 51 H3
Swan La RW/EYN OX29 6 B4
Swan St OXN/BOT/CM OX2 33 E5
RW/EYN OX29 22 C4
Sweet Briar MCHM/KBPZ OX13 58 C4
Sweetmans Rd
OXN/BOT/CM OX2 39 F2
Swift Cl COW/LTMR OX4 51 H3
Swinbourne Rd COW/LTMR OX4 50 D2
Swinburne Rd ABGD OX14 61 E2
COW/LTMR OX4 41 F3
Swinford Bridge (Toll)
RW/EYN OX29 23 E5
Swingburn Pl WITNEY OX28 21 E3
Sworford La WHLY OX33 45 H3
Sycamore Cl MCHM/KBPZ OX13 59 H1
WITNEY OX28 21 G1
Sycamore Crs OX/KTN OX1 50 A5
Sycamore Rd OXN/BOT/CM OX2 39 F2
Sympson Cl ABGD OX14 60 C4

T

Tackley Pl OXN/BOT/CM OX2 33 F2
Taggs Ga HEAD OX3 35 H2
Talbot Rd OXN/BOT/CM OX2 26 A1
Tanners La RW/EYN OX29 22 D4
Tannery Ct ABGD OX14 60 C3
Taphouse Av WITNEY OX28 21 F1
Tarragon Dr COW/LTMR OX4 51 H3
Tatham Rd ABGD OX14 60 D1
Taverner Pl HEAD OX3 34 B2
Tawney St COW/LTMR OX4 41 G1
Teal Cl COW/LTMR OX4 51 H3
Templar Rd OXN/BOT/CM OX2 26 B2
Templars Cl WHLY OX33 44 C1
Temple Rd COW/LTMR OX4 42 A3
Temple St COW/LTMR OX4 3 J6
The Tennis RW/EYN OX29 23 G1
Tennyson Dr ABGD OX14 60 A5
Tern Wk COW/LTMR OX4 51 G3
Terrington Cl ABGD OX14 56 A5
Tetbury Dr WITNEY OX28 20 B2
Thackley End OXN/BOT/CM OX2 33 F1
Thame La ABGD OX14 64 A1
Thames Pth ABGD OX14 64 C4
OXN/BOT/CM OX2 33 E4
RW/EYN OX29 24 B2
Thames St ABGD OX14 60 D4
OX/KTN OX1 2 E6
RW/EYN OX29 22 C4
Thames Vw ABGD OX14 61 E3
Thames View Rd
COW/LTMR OX4 50 B2
Thesiger Rd ABGD OX14 60 D2
Third Acre Ri OXN/BOT/CM OX2 38 D1
Thistlecroft Cl ABGD OX14 56 B5
Thistle Dr COW/LTMR OX4 52 A2
Thomson Ter COW/LTMR OX4 50 C2
Thornbury Rd RW/EYN OX29 22 B4
Thorncliffe Rd
OXN/BOT/CM OX2 26 B5
Thorne Cl KID OX5 9 G4
Thorney Leys WITNEY OX28 20 C5
Thornhill Wk ABGD OX14 60 C1
Three Corners Rd
COW/LTMR OX4 52 A2
Three Fields Rd HEAD OX3 42 C2
Thrift Pl COW/LTMR OX4 51 H2
Thrupp La ABGD OX14 61 H2
Thurston Cl ABGD OX14 60 C4
Tidmarsh La OX/KTN OX1 2 C4
Tilbury La OXN/BOT/CM OX2 32 A4
Tilehouse Cl HEAD OX3 35 G3
Tilgarsley Rd RW/EYN OX29 22 B3
Timothy Wy COW/LTMR OX4 51 H2
Titup Hall Dr HEAD OX3 35 G5
Tollgate Rd ABGD OX14 63 H3
Toot Hill Butts HEAD OX3 35 H3
Tower Cl ABGD OX14 60 B4
MCHM/KBPZ OX13 58 D4
Tower Hl WITNEY OX28 20 D3
Town Furlong
MCHM/KBPZ OX13 46 A4
Town Furze HEAD OX3 42 B2
The Town Gn KID OX5 10 B4
Townsend ABGD OX14 60 D5
Townsend Sq COW/LTMR OX4 41 F3
Toynbee Cl OXN/BOT/CM OX2 39 F2
Trafford Rd HEAD OX3 35 G3
Tree Close Bay COW/LTMR OX4 41 G5
Treeground Pl KID OX5 10 A5
Tree La COW/LTMR OX4 41 G5
Trefoil Pl COW/LTMR OX4 52 A2
Trendell Pl ABGD OX14 60 C1
Trevor Pl COW/LTMR OX4 41 H4
Trinity Cl ABGD OX14 56 B5
Trinity Rd HEAD OX3 35 G4
Trinity St OX/KTN OX1 2 C6
Troy Cl HEAD OX3 42 C2
Tucker Rd COW/LTMR OX4 51 G1
Tudor Ct OXN/BOT/CM OX2 38 C1
The Tuer RW/EYN OX29 22 C4
Turberville Cl ABGD OX14 60 C4
Turl St OX/KTN OX1 * 2 E3
Turnagain La ABGD OX14 60 D4
Turn Again La OX/KTN OX1 2 D5
Turner Cl COW/LTMR OX4 42 B3
Turner Rd ABGD OX14 60 B5
Turners Cl ABGD OX14 57 F5
Turnpike Rd OXN/BOT/CM OX2 38 D3
Twelve Acre Dr ABGD OX14 56 B4
Tyndale Pl WHLY OX33 45 E1
Tyndale Rd COW/LTMR OX4 3 J5
Tyne Rd MCHM/KBPZ OX13 55 F4

U

Ulfgar Rd OXN/BOT/CM OX2 25 H3
Underhill Circ HEAD OX3 35 H2
Union St COW/LTMR OX4 41 F1
WDSTK OX20 4 D4
Union Wy WITNEY OX28 20 D3
Upland Park Rd
OXN/BOT/CM OX2 26 A3
Upper Brook Hl WDSTK OX20 4 D4
Upper Campsfield Rd KID OX5 5 G5
Upper Fisher Rw OX/KTN OX1 2 B3
Upper Meadow HEAD OX3 35 G5
Upper Rd OX/KTN OX1 49 H2
Upton Cl ABGD OX14 61 E1
COW/LTMR OX4 51 E2
Upway Rd HEAD OX3 34 D1

V

Valence Crs WITNEY OX28 20 B3
Valentia Rd HEAD OX3 34 D4
Vale Rd WITNEY OX28 20 C3
Valley Rd WHLY OX33 43 H3
Vanbrugh Cl WDSTK OX20 4 C3
Van-dieman's La
COW/LTMR OX4 51 E1
Vanner Rd WITNEY OX28 21 G1
Varsity Pl OX/KTN OX1 * 40 D4
Venables Cl OXN/BOT/CM OX2 33 F3
Venneit Cl OXN/BOT/CM OX2 2 A1
Verbena Wy COW/LTMR OX4 51 G3
Vermont Dr WDSTK OX20 4 C3
Vernon Av OXN/BOT/CM OX2 39 G3
Vetch Pl COW/LTMR OX4 51 H2
Vicarage Cl COW/LTMR OX4 50 D2
Vicarage La OX/KTN OX1 40 C3
Vicarage Rd KID OX5 10 B4
OX/KTN OX1 40 C3
Victoria Ct OX/KTN OX1 * 2 D3
Victoria Rd ABGD OX14 60 B3
OXN/BOT/CM OX2 26 B3
Victor St OXN/BOT/CM OX2 2 B1
Villeboys Cl ABGD OX14 61 G2
Villiers La COW/LTMR OX4 41 G5
Viner Cl WITNEY OX28 21 G1
Vineyard ABGD OX14 60 D3
Violet Wy COW/LTMR OX4 51 G4
Virginia Wy ABGD OX14 62 D1

W

Wadard's Meadow
WITNEY OX28 21 G3
Waine Rush Vw WITNEY OX28 21 F3
Walkers Cl RW/EYN OX29 13 G2
The Walk KID OX5 11 H4
Wallace Cl ABGD OX14 60 C5
Walnut Cl WITNEY OX28 20 D4
Walton Crs OXN/BOT/CM OX2 2 C1
Walton La OX/KTN OX1 2 C1
Walton Manor Ct
OXN/BOT/CM OX2 33 F3
Walton St OXN/BOT/CM OX2 2 B1
Walton Well Rd
OXN/BOT/CM OX2 33 E3
Warbler Wk COW/LTMR OX4 51 G3
Warburg Crs COW/LTMR OX4 51 H1
Warnborough Rd
OXN/BOT/CM OX2 33 F2
Warneford La HEAD OX3 34 D5
Warneford Rd COW/LTMR OX4 41 G1
Warren Crs HEAD OX3 35 F5
The Warren ABGD OX14 61 F2
Warwick Cl ABGD OX14 61 E2
Warwick St COW/LTMR OX4 41 F2
Wastie's Orch RW/EYN OX29 6 B4
Water Eaton La KID OX5 18 A1
Water Eaton Rd
OXN/BOT/CM OX2 26 C3
Waterford Rd RW/EYN OX29 21 H2
Watermead KID OX5 10 C5
Watermill Wy HEAD OX3 36 A2
Watery La ABGD OX14 65 H1
Watlington Rd COW/LTMR OX4 51 H1
STAD OX44 52 B3
Watson Crs MCHM/KBPZ OX13 47 G5
Waverley Av KID OX5 10 C5
Waxes Cl ABGD OX14 56 C5
Wayfaring Cl COW/LTMR OX4 51 G4
Waynflete Rd HEAD OX3 35 H2
Weavers Cl WITNEY OX28 21 E4
Webb's Cl OXN/BOT/CM OX2 25 F3
Webb's Wy KID OX5 10 B4
Websters Cl RW/EYN OX29 13 G2
Weirs La OX/KTN OX1 40 D4
Welch Wy WITNEY OX28 21 E3
Weldon Rd HEAD OX3 34 B2
Welford Gdns ABGD OX14 56 A5
Welland Cl MCHM/KBPZ OX13 55 E5
Wellesbourne Cl ABGD OX14 61 F2
Wellington Pl OX/KTN OX1 2 D2
Wellington Sq OX/KTN OX1 2 C1
Wellington St OXN/BOT/CM OX2 2 B1
Wenman Rd WITNEY OX28 20 C3
Wentworth Rd
OXN/BOT/CM OX2 26 B3
Wesley Cl COW/LTMR OX4 51 G2
Wesley Wk WITNEY OX28 * 21 F3
West Av ABGD OX14 56 A5
Westbury Crs COW/LTMR OX4 41 H5
Westcote Cl WITNEY OX28 20 B4
West End RW/EYN OX29 6 A1
WITNEY OX28 21 F1
Western By-Pass Rd
OXN/BOT/CM OX2 32 A2
Western Rd OX/KTN OX1 2 E7
Westfield Cl COW/LTMR OX4 41 H3
Westfield Rd WHLY OX33 37 G5
WITNEY OX28 21 E1
Westfields ABGD OX14 60 B2
Westlands Dr HEAD OX3 34 D1
Westlands Wy WDSTK OX20 4 C3
Westminster Wy
OXN/BOT/CM OX2 39 F1
Westrup Cl HEAD OX3 34 B3
West Saint Helen St ABGD OX14 60 D3
West St OXN/BOT/CM OX2 33 E5
West Wy OXN/BOT/CM OX2 32 A5
Westwood Rd RW/EYN OX29 20 A2
Wesy Quay ABGD OX14 63 F1
Weyland Rd HEAD OX3 35 G4
Wharf Cl ABGD OX14 60 C4
Wharton Rd HEAD OX3 35 F3
Wheatcroft Cl ABGD OX14 56 A5
Wheatley Br WHLY OX33 45 G2
Wheatley Rd KID OX5 11 H5
STAD OX44 53 E2
WHLY OX33 37 F2
Whitecross MCHM/KBPZ OX13 55 E2
White Hill La OX/KTN OX1 47 G3
Whitehorns Wy ABGD OX14 62 A4
Whitehouse Cl
MCHM/KBPZ OX13 60 A1
Whitehouse Rd OX/KTN OX1 2 D7
Whitelock Rd ABGD OX14 60 D1
White Rd COW/LTMR OX4 42 C4
Whites Forge
MCHM/KBPZ OX13 46 A4
White's La ABGD OX14 56 D4
White Wy KID OX5 10 A5
Whitson Pl COW/LTMR OX4 41 G2
Whitworth Pl OXN/BOT/CM OX2 2 A1
Wick Cl ABGD OX14 56 C5
HEAD OX3 35 G2
Wilberforce St HEAD OX3 35 F4
Wilcote Rd HEAD OX3 35 H2
Wilcote Vw RW/EYN OX29 12 C1
Wildmoor Ga ABGD OX14 60 B1
Wilkins Rd COW/LTMR OX4 42 B4
William Kimber Crs HEAD OX3 35 G3
William Orchard Cl HEAD OX3 35 E2
Williamson Wy COW/LTMR OX4 50 C2
William St HEAD OX3 34 B3
Willow Brook ABGD OX14 60 B3
Willow Cl KID OX5 16 C2
STAD OX44 52 C2
Willows Edge RW/EYN OX29 22 B4
The Willows WITNEY OX28 21 G2
Willow Tree Cl
MCHM/KBPZ OX13 60 A1
Willow Wy ABGD OX14 50 A5
KID OX5 9 E5
Wilmot Cl WITNEY OX28 20 D5
Wilsdon Wy KID OX5 9 H4
Wilsham Rd ABGD OX14 60 D4
Wilson Pl COW/LTMR OX4 * 3 K4
Winchester Rd
OXN/BOT/CM OX2 33 F2
Windale Av COW/LTMR OX4 51 G2
Windmill Cl RW/EYN OX29 12 B3
Windmill Hts RW/EYN OX29 12 B2
Windmill La WHLY OX33 44 B2
Windmill Rd HEAD OX3 35 F4
RW/EYN OX29 12 B2
Windrush Cl WITNEY OX28 20 C2
Windrush Park Rd
RW/EYN OX29 20 A2
Windrush Valley Rd
WITNEY OX28 20 C2
Windrush Wy ABGD OX14 61 F1
Windsor Crs HEAD OX3 34 A1
Windsor St HEAD OX3 35 F4
Wingate Cl COW/LTMR OX4 51 G1
The Winnyards
OXN/BOT/CM OX2 38 A5
Winsmore La ABGD OX14 60 D3
Winston Cl KID OX5 17 G1
Winterborne Rd ABGD OX14 60 B3
Wise Av KID OX5 9 H4
Witan Pk WITNEY OX28 * 21 F5
Witan Wy WITNEY OX28 21 F4
Withington Ct ABGD OX14 60 D3
Witney Rd RW/EYN OX29 6 A4
RW/EYN OX29 22 B3
Wolsey Ct KID OX5 8 C2
Wolsey Rd OXN/BOT/CM OX2 26 B2
Wolvercote Gn
OXN/BOT/CM OX2 25 G3
Woodbine Pl OX/KTN OX1 2 B4
Woodcote Wy ABGD OX14 63 E1
Woodcroft OX/KTN OX1 50 A3
Wood Farm Rd HEAD OX3 42 C1
Woodford Ml WITNEY OX28 * 21 E2
Woodgreen Hl WITNEY OX28 21 F2
Woodhouse Wy
COW/LTMR OX4 41 G4
Woodlands RW/EYN OX29 13 G1
Woodlands Cl HEAD OX3 34 D3
Woodlands Rd HEAD OX3 34 D3
WITNEY OX28 21 G1
Woodley Cl ABGD OX14 55 H4
Woodpecker Gn
COW/LTMR OX4 51 H3
Woodperry Rd HEAD OX3 29 F1
Woodruff Cl COW/LTMR OX4 51 H2
Woodside RW/EYN OX29 12 C2
Woodstock Cl
OXN/BOT/CM OX2 26 A3
Woodstock Rd KID OX5 17 F4
OXN/BOT/CM OX2 33 F1
WDSTK OX20 8 C1
WITNEY OX28 21 G1
Woodstock Rd West KID OX5 8 D4
Wootton Rd MCHM/KBPZ OX13 55 F3
Worcester Pl OX/KTN OX1 2 C2
Worcester St OX/KTN OX1 2 C3
Wordsworth Rd ABGD OX14 60 B5
Wren Cl WHLY OX33 44 D1
Wren Rd OXN/BOT/CM OX2 26 C3
Wrightson Cl WHLY OX33 43 G3
Wroslyn Rd RW/EYN OX29 13 G4
Wyatt Rd OXN/BOT/CM OX2 26 B2
Wychwood Cl WITNEY OX28 20 C3
Wychwood La HEAD OX3 36 A4
Wykeham Crs COW/LTMR OX4 41 H5
Wylie Cl HEAD OX3 42 B1
Wynbush Rd COW/LTMR OX4 50 C1
Wyndham Wy
OXN/BOT/CM OX2 26 A3
Wyndyke Furlong ABGD OX14 60 A2
Wytham Cl RW/EYN OX29 22 C3
Wytham St OX/KTN OX1 40 D4
Wytham Vw RW/EYN OX29 22 C3

Y

Yarnell's Hl OXN/BOT/CM OX2 39 F2
Yarnell's Rd OXN/BOT/CM OX2 39 G1
Yarnton Ct KID OX5 10 A5
Yarnton La KID OX5 17 F2
Yarnton Rd KID OX5 17 F1
RW/EYN OX29 15 H5
Yeats Cl COW/LTMR OX4 42 C3
Yeftly Dr COW/LTMR OX4 50 C3
Yeld Hall Rd ABGD OX14 56 B5
Yewtree Ms ABGD OX14 60 D3
York Av HEAD OX3 35 G5
York Pl COW/LTMR OX4 3 J4
York Rd HEAD OX3 35 G4
Ypres Wy ABGD OX14 60 B1

Abingdon Airfield
MCHM/KBPZ OX13 ....54 C3
Abingdon Four Pillars Hotel
ABGD OX14 ....59 H4
Abingdon Hospital
ABGD OX14 ....60 A3
Abingdon Museum
ABGD OX14 ....60 D5
Abingdon RFC
ABGD OX14 ....63 E1
Abingdon School
ABGD OX14 ....60 C3
Abingdon & Witney College
ABGD OX14 ....60 C1
All Souls College
OX/KTN OX1 ....3 F3
Appleton CE Primary School
MCHM/KBPZ OX13 ....46 A4
Artworks School of
Art & Design
COW/LTMR OX4 ....41 F2
Ashmolean Museum of
Art & Archaeology
OX/KTN OX1 ....2 D2
Avenue Three
WITNEY OX28 ....21 F5
Avenue Two
WITNEY OX28 ....21 F5
The Balkan Lodge Hotel
COW/LTMR OX4 ....41 F3
Balliol College
OX/KTN OX1 ....2 E3
Banbury Road Medical Centre
OXN/BOT/CM OX2 ....26 B5
Banbury Road North
Sports Ground
OXN/BOT/CM OX2 ....26 A1
Bartholomew School
RW/EYN OX29 ....22 B3
Bate Collection of Musical
Instruments
OX/KTN OX1 ....2 E5
Batt CE Primary School
WITNEY OX28 ....21 F3
Bayards Hill Primary School
HEAD OX3 ....35 H3
The Bear Hotel
WDSTK OX20 ....4 C4
Bessels Leigh School
MCHM/KBPZ OX13 ....46 C5
Blackbird Leys Health Centre
COW/LTMR OX4 ....51 G2
Blackbird Leys Leisure Centre
COW/LTMR OX4 ....51 G2
Bladon CE Primary School
WDSTK OX20 ....7 H3
The Blake CE Primary School
WITNEY OX28 ....21 G3
Blenheim Palace
WDSTK OX20 ....4 C1
Bodleian Library
OX/KTN OX1 ....3 F3
Botley County Primary School
OXN/BOT/CM OX2 ....32 B5
Botley Medical Centre
OXN/BOT/CM OX2 ....32 A5
Boundary Business Park
STAD OX44 ....53 F1
Bowling Alley
COW/LTMR OX4 ....51 F3
Brasenose College
OX/KTN OX1 ....3 F3
Brasenose College Sports
Ground *OX/KTN* OX1 ....40 C3
Buckland University College
HEAD OX3 ....34 C3
Bury Knowle Health Centre
HEAD OX3 ....35 F3
Caldecott Primary School
ABGD OX14 ....60 B5
Carfax Tower
OX/KTN OX1 ....2 D3
Carswell Primary School
ABGD OX14 ....60 C3
Chandlings Manor School
MCHM/KBPZ OX13 ....49 F5
Cheney School
HEAD OX3 ....34 D5
Cherwell College
OX/KTN OX1 ....2 C4
The Cherwell School
OXN/BOT/CM OX2 ....26 C5
Chiltern Business Centre
COW/LTMR OX4 ....42 C5
Christ Church Cathedral School
OX/KTN OX1 ....3 F5
Christ Church College
OX/KTN OX1 ....3 F5
Christ Church College &
Cathedral *OX/KTN* OX1 ....3 F5
Christ Church Sports Ground
OX/KTN OX1 ....3 H6
Church Cowley St James
First School *COW/LTMR* OX4 .42 A5
Churchill Hospital
HEAD OX3 ....42 A1
Clarendon Centre
OX/KTN OX1 ....2 D3
Clifton Hampden CE
Primary School *ABGD* OX14 ...65 H1
Cogges Manor Farm Museum
WITNEY OX28 ....21 G3
College of Further Education
COW/LTMR OX4 ....51 G2
Column of Victory
WDSTK OX20 ....4 B3
Combe CE Primary School
RW/EYN OX29 ....6 A1
Corpus Christi College
OX/KTN OX1 ....3 F4
Cothill House Preparatory
School *MCHM/KBPZ* OX13 ....54 A3
Cotswold Lodge Hotel
OXN/BOT/CM OX2 ....33 G2
County Hall
OX/KTN OX1 ....2 C4

County Trading Estate
COW/LTMR OX4 ....42 D5
Covered Market
OX/KTN OX1 ....2 E3
Cowley Business Centre
COW/LTMR OX4 ....51 H1
Culham Parochial CE
Primary School
ABGD OX14 ....63 H2
Cumnor CE Primary School
OXN/BOT/CM OX2 ....38 A4
Cutteslowe Primary School
OXN/BOT/CM OX2 ....26 C2
Deer Park Medical Centre
WITNEY OX28 ....20 B3
Denman College
MCHM/KBPZ OX13 ....58 C4
Dr Souths CE Primary School
KID OX5 ....11 H4
D'Overbroecks College
OXN/BOT/CM OX2 ....26 B5
OXN/BOT/CM OX2 ....33 G2
Dragon School
OXN/BOT/CM OX2 ....33 G2
Drayton Primary School
ABGD OX14 ....62 B3
Dry Sandford County
Primary School
MCHM/KBPZ OX13 ....54 B1
Dunmore Infant &
Junior School *ABGD* OX14 ...55 H5
Eagle Industrial Estate
WITNEY OX28 ....21 E4
Eastgate Hotel
OX/KTN OX1 ....3 C4
East Oxford Primary School
COW/LTMR OX4 ....41 F1
Edward Feild Primary School
KID OX5 ....17 H1
Emmanuel Christian School
COW/LTMR OX4 ....50 D2
Exeter College
OX/KTN OX1 ....2 E3
Exeter College Sports Ground
HEAD OX3 ....34 A2
Express by Holiday Inn
COW/LTMR OX4 ....51 F3
Eye Hospital Radcliffe
Infirmary *OXN/BOT/CM* OX2 .33 F3
Eynsham County Primary
School *RW/EYN* OX29 ....22 D5
Eynsham Medical Centre
RW/EYN OX29 ....22 C4
The Feathers Hotel
WDSTK OX20 ....4 C4
Ferry Sports Centre
OXN/BOT/CM OX2 ....26 B5
Fitzharrys School
ABGD OX14 ....60 D1
Forest Farm Oxford
Montessori School
HEAD OX3 ....28 A1
Freeland CE Primary School
RW/EYN OX29 ....13 C1
Frilford Heath Golf Club
MCHM/KBPZ OX13 ....58 A1
Garsington CE Primary School
COW/LTMR OX4 ....53 E2
Garsington Sports Club
COW/LTMR OX4 ....53 E2
Golden Cross Shopping Centre
OX/KTN OX1 ....2 E4
Gosford All Blacks RFC
KID OX5 ....17 H3
Gosford Hill Medical Centre
KID OX5 ....17 H1
Gosford Hill School
KID OX5 ....17 H1
Green College
OXN/BOT/CM OX2 ....33 F3
Hanborough Business Park
RW/EYN OX29 ....7 E4
Hanborough Manor CE School
RW/EYN OX29 ....6 B4
Harris Manchester College
OX/KTN OX1 ....3 F2
Hartwell Academy
MCHM/KBPZ OX13 ....47 E3
Hawkwell House Hotel
COW/LTMR OX4 ....41 F5
Headington Junior School
HEAD OX3 ....35 E4
Headington School
HEAD OX3 ....34 C4
HEAD OX3 ....34 D4
Headington Senior School
HEAD OX3 ....34 D4
The Henry Box School
WITNEY OX28 ....21 E4
Hertford College
OX/KTN OX1 ....3 F3
Hertford College Sports Ground
HEAD OX3 ....34 A2
Hill End Residential & Field
Study Centre
OXN/BOT/CM OX2 ....31 F4
Hinksey Business Centre
OXN/BOT/CM OX2 ....32 B5
Hinksey Heights Golf Club
OX/KTN OX1 ....40 A4
Hinksey Pool
OX/KTN OX1 ....40 C3
Holiday Inn
OXN/BOT/CM OX2 ....17 H5
Hollow Way Medical Centre
COW/LTMR OX4 ....42 B4
Holywell Business Centre
OXN/BOT/CM OX2 ....2 A6
Horspath Athletics Track
COW/LTMR OX4 ....43 E3
Horspath CE Primary School
WHLY OX33 ....43 G2
Iffley Mead School
COW/LTMR OX4 ....41 F4

Institute of Virology &
Environmental Microbiology
OXN/BOT/CM OX2 ....3 G1
Isis Business Centre
COW/LTMR OX4 ....42 D5
Isis Clinic
COW/LTMR OX4 ....41 F5
Jericho Health Centre
OXN/BOT/CM OX2 ....33 E3
Jesus College
OX/KTN OX1 ....2 E3
Jesus College Sports Ground
COW/LTMR OX4 ....41 H2
The John Henry Newman CE
Primary School
COW/LTMR OX4 ....50 D2
John Mason School
ABGD OX14 ....60 C2
John Radcliffe Hospital
HEAD OX3 ....35 E2
John Radcliffe Hospital -
Cardiac Centre
HEAD OX3 ....34 D2
John Radcliffe Hospital -
New Children's Hospital
HEAD OX3 ....34 D2
John Radcliffe Hospital -
Women's Centre
HEAD OX3 ....35 E3
John Watson School
WHLY OX33 ....44 C1
Jordan Hill Business Park
OXN/BOT/CM OX2 ....26 A1
Joscas Preparatory School
MCHM/KBPZ OX13 ....58 A3
Keble College
OX/KTN OX1 ....2 E1
Kennington Health Centre
OX/KTN OX1 ....50 A3
Kidlington & Gosford
Sports Centre
KID OX5 ....17 H1
Kidlington Health Centre
KID OX5 ....10 A5
Kingfisher School
ABGD OX14 ....60 C4
ABGD OX14 ....61 F2
Kings Arms Hotel
WDSTK OX20 ....4 C4
Kings Meadow Industrial
Estate *OXN/BOT/CM* OX2 ......39 H1
Kings School Oxford
COW/LTMR OX4 ....42 A3
The Kings School Seniors
WITNEY OX28 ....21 F3
Lady Margaret Hall (University
of Oxford College)
OXN/BOT/CM OX2 ....33 H2
The Langford Business Park
KID OX5 ....9 F3
Larkmead School
ABGD OX14 ....60 A2
Larkrise First School
COW/LTMR OX4 ....41 G3
Linacre College
OXN/BOT/CM OX2 ....33 H3
Lincoln College
OX/KTN OX1 ....2 E3
Lincoln College Sports Ground
COW/LTMR OX4 ....41 H2
Linton Lodge Hotel
OXN/BOT/CM OX2 ....33 G1
Littleworth Industrial Estate
WHLY OX33 ....44 B1
Long Furlong Medical Centre
ABGD OX14 ....56 A4
Long Furlong Primary School
ABGD OX14 ....56 A4
Long Wittenham CE Primary
School *ABGD* OX14 ....65 H5
Mabel Prichard School
COW/LTMR OX4 ....50 D2
Madley Brook Primary School
WITNEY OX28 ....21 H1
Magdalen College
OX/KTN OX1 ....3 G5
Magdalen College School
COW/LTMR OX4 ....3 J5
Magdalen College Sports
Ground *HEAD* OX3 ....3 K2
Manor Hospital
HEAD OX3 ....35 E3
Manor House Hotel
COW/LTMR OX4 ....41 F2
Manor Preparatory School
MCHM/KBPZ OX13 ....60 A1
Mansfield College
OX/KTN OX1 ....3 F1
Marcham CE Primary School
MCHM/KBPZ OX13 ....58 D4
Marcham Road Health Centre
ABGD OX14 ....60 A3
The Marlborough Arms Hotel
WDSTK OX20 ....4 D4
Marlborough School
WDSTK OX20 ....5 E4
Marston Health Centre
HEAD OX3 ....34 C1
Martyrs Memorial
OX/KTN OX1 ....2 E2
Matthew Arnold School
OXN/BOT/CM OX2 ....39 E2
Merton College
OX/KTN OX1 ....3 G4
Millbrook Industrial Estate
WITNEY OX28 ....21 F5
Modern Art Oxford
OX/KTN OX1 ....2 E4
Museum of Oxford
OX/KTN OX1 ....2 E4
Museum of the History
of Science *OX/KTN* OX1 ....2 E3
New Bodleian Library
OX/KTN OX1 ....2 E2

New College
OX/KTN OX1 ....3 F2
New College School
OX/KTN OX1 ....3 F2
New Hinksey CE Primary School
COW/LTMR OX4 ....40 C3
New Marston Primary School
HEAD OX3 ....34 C1
New Theatre
OX/KTN OX1 ....2 D3
Northern House School
OXN/BOT/CM OX2 ....26 A4
Northfield School
COW/LTMR OX4 ....51 F3
North Hinksey CE School
OXN/BOT/CM OX2 ....39 G1
North Kidlington Primary
School *KID* OX5 ....9 H4
North Leigh Business Park
RW/EYN OX29 ....12 C1
North Leigh CE Primary School
RW/EYN OX29 ....12 B2
North Leigh FC
RW/EYN OX29 ....12 D2
North Oxford Golf Club
OXN/BOT/CM OX2 ....18 A5
North Oxford Medical Centre
OXN/BOT/CM OX2 ....33 F1
Northway Health Centre
HEAD OX3 ....34 D1
Northway Sports Centre
HEAD OX3 ....34 C1
Nuffield College
OX/KTN OX1 ....2 C3
Nuffield Health Centre
WITNEY OX28 ....21 E5
Nuffield Industrial Estate
COW/LTMR OX4 ....51 E2
Nuffield Orthopaedic Hospital
HEAD OX3 ....35 F4
Oakfield Industrial Estate
RW/EYN OX29 ....22 B5
Oasis Park
RW/EYN OX29 ....22 B5
Odeon Cinema
OX/KTN OX1 ....2 D3
Old Fire Station Theatre
OX/KTN OX1 ....2 D3
The Old Gaol Leisure Centre
ABGD OX14 ....60 D4
The Open University
OXN/BOT/CM OX2 ....48 B5
Orchard Meadow First School
COW/LTMR OX4 ....51 G2
Oriel College
OX/KTN OX1 ....3 F4
Oriel College Sports Ground
COW/LTMR OX4 ....41 H1
Ormerod School
HEAD OX3 ....36 A3
Osney Cemetery
OXN/BOT/CM OX2 ....2 A5
Osney Mead Industrial Estate
OXN/BOT/CM OX2 ....2 B6
Our Lady of Lourdes RC
Primary School
WITNEY OX28 ....20 C4
Our Ladys Catholic Primary
School *COW/LTMR* OX4 ....42 A4
Our Ladys Convent Junior
School *ABGD* OX14 ....61 E2
Our Ladys Convent Senior
School *ABGD* OX14 ....61 E2
Oxford Brookes University
HEAD OX3 ....34 C3
HEAD OX3 ....34 C4
HEAD OX3 ....34 D5
HEAD OX3 ....35 E4
Oxford Brookes University
(Harcourt Hill Campus)
OXN/BOT/CM OX2 ....39 F3
Oxford Brookes University
(Wheatley Campus)
WHLY OX33 ....45 E1
Oxford Brookes University
Sports Centre
HEAD OX3 ....34 C5
Oxford Business Centre
OX/KTN OX1 ....2 B4
OX/KTN OX1 ....2 B5
Oxford Bus Museum
RW/EYN OX29 ....7 E4
Oxford Castle Mound & Prison
OX/KTN OX1 ....2 C4
Oxford City FC
HEAD OX3 ....34 C1
Oxford College of Further
Education *OX/KTN* OX1 ....2 C4
Oxford Community Health
COW/LTMR OX4 ....41 G4
Oxford Crematorium
HEAD OX3 ....35 H1
Oxford Crown & County Court
OX/KTN OX1 ....2 E6
Oxford High School GDST
OXN/BOT/CM OX2 ....26 C5
The Oxford Hotel
OXN/BOT/CM OX2 ....25 G2
Oxford Ice Rink
OX/KTN OX1 ....2 C6
Oxford (Kidlington) Airport
OXN/BOT/CM OX2 ....9 E2
Oxford Magistrates Court
OX/KTN OX1 ....2 D5
Oxford Marathon Rugby Club
COW/LTMR OX4 ....43 E3
Oxford Motor Park
KID OX5 ....9 F3
Oxford Old Boys RFC
OXN/BOT/CM OX2 ....26 C5
The Oxford Playhouse Theatre
OX/KTN OX1 ....2 D3

Oxford Retail Park
COW/LTMR OX4 ....35 E4
COW/LTMR OX4 ....35 E4
Oxford RFC
OXN/BOT/CM OX2 ....26 C5
Oxford School
COW/LTMR OX4 ....42 C5
Oxford Science Park
COW/LTMR OX4 ....52 C5
Oxfordshire Fire Service
Headquarters *KID* OX5 ....17 F4
The Oxfordshire Museum
WDSTK OX20 ....4 D4
Oxford Spires Business Park
KID OX5 ....17 F4
Oxford Spires Four Pillars
Hotel *OX/KTN* OX1 ....3 J5
Oxford Stadium
COW/LTMR OX4 ....51 H2
The Oxford Story
OX/KTN OX1 ....2 E3
Oxford Thames Four Pillars
Hotel *COW/LTMR* OX4 ....51 H2
Oxford Town Hall
OX/KTN OX1 ....2 D4
Oxford Tutorial College
OX/KTN OX1 ....2 E5
Oxford United FC (The Kassam
Stadium) *COW/LTMR* OX4 ....52 C5
Oxford University
OXN/BOT/CM OX2 ....33 H2
Oxford University Museum
of Natural History
OXN/BOT/CM OX2 ....3 G1
Oxford University Press
OXN/BOT/CM OX2 ....33 E3
Oxford University RFC
COW/LTMR OX4 ....41 H2
Oxford University Sports
Centre *COW/LTMR* OX4 ....41 H2
Oxford University Track
COW/LTMR OX4 ....41 H2
OXSRAD *HEAD* OX3 ....35 F4
Ozone Leisure Park
COW/LTMR OX4 ....52 D5
Paradise Street Business
Centre *OX/KTN* OX1 ....2 C4
Park Hospital for Children
HEAD OX3 ....35 F3
The Park Sports Centre
WHLY OX33 ....44 C1
Peachcroft Shopping Centre
ABGD OX14 ....56 C4
Peers Upper School
COW/LTMR OX4 ....51 H3
Pegasus Primary School
COW/LTMR OX4 ....51 F2
Pembroke College
OX/KTN OX1 ....2 D5
Pendon Museum
ABGD OX14 ....65 H5
Phoenix Picture House
Cinema *OXN/BOT/CM* OX2 ....33 F3
Pitt Rivers Museum
OXN/BOT/CM OX2 ....3 G1
The Plain
OX/KTN OX1 ....3 H5
Plater College
HEAD OX3 ....34 A3
Queens College
OX/KTN OX1 ....3 G4
OXN/BOT/CM OX2 ....3 G4
Queens College Sports Ground
OX/KTN OX1 ....3 G4
Queens Dyke County Primary
School *WITNEY* OX28 ....20 C4
Radcliffe Camera
OX/KTN OX1 ....2 F3
Radcliffe Infirmary
OXN/BOT/CM OX2 ....33 F2
The Radford Track
ABGD OX14 ....60 D4
Radley CE Primary School
ABGD OX14 ....62 C5
Radley College
ABGD OX14 ....62 C4
Radley Road Industrial Estate
ABGD OX14 ....61 F3
The Randolph Hotel
OX/KTN OX1 ....2 D2
Regents Park College
OX/KTN OX1 ....2 E2
Rhodes House
OX/KTN OX1 ....3 F2
Ripon College
STAD OX44 ....54 D1
Rose Hill Primary School
COW/LTMR OX4 ....51 G3
Rush Common Primary School
ABGD OX14 ....60 C4
Ruskin College
OXN/BOT/CM OX2 ....33 H1
Rye St Anthony School
HEAD OX3 ....34 C5
Said Business School
OX/KTN OX1 ....2 C3
St Aldates Church
OX/KTN OX1 ....2 D5
St Aldates College
OX/KTN OX1 ....2 C6
St Aloysius RC First School
OXN/BOT/CM OX2 ....33 F1
St Andrews CE School
HEAD OX3 ....34 D2
St Annes College
OXN/BOT/CM OX2 ....33 F1
St Barnabas' CE First School
OXN/BOT/CM OX2 ....33 E3
St Bartholomews Medical
Centre *COW/LTMR* OX4 ....41 H4
St Catherines College
OX/KTN OX1 ....3 H2

istophers CE First School
W/LTMR OX4 ....42 A4
res Oxford
N/BOT/CM OX2 ....33 F1
oss College
/KTN OX1 ....2 D2
pe's CE First School
/KTN OX1 ....2 D7
mund Hall
/KTN OX1 ....3 G3
munds RC Primary
hool ABGD OX14 ....61 G2
wards School
N/BOT/CM OX2 ....26 B5
orges Tower
W/LTMR OX4 ....42 C3
ancis CE First School
/KTN OX1 ....2 C4
egory The Great RC
condary School
W/LTMR OX4 ....41 F4
W/LTMR OX4 ....41 G3
das College
/KTN OX1 ....3 H5
ghes College
N/BOT/CM OX2 ....33 F2
nn Fisher RC Primary
hool COW/LTMR OX4 ....51 F1
nns College
/KTN OX1 ....2 E2
sephs Catholic Primary
AD OX3 ....34 C2
arys Infant School
ITNEY OX28 ....21 F4
chaels CE Primary School
AD OX3 ....34 B3
cholas Primary School
AD OX3 ....34 A1
colas CE Primary School
GD OX14 ....60 D2
eters CE (A) Primary
hool RW/EYN OX29 ....23 G1
eters College
/KTN OX1 ....2 D3
vithuns CE Primary
hool OX/KTN OX1 ....50 A3
oomas More RC Primary
hool KID OX5 ....17 G1

Ss Mary and John CE First
School COW/LTMR OX4 ....41 G2
Ss Philip and James CE
Primary School
OXN/BOT/CM OX2 ....33 E2
Sandhills Primary School
HEAD OX3 ....36 B2
Saxon Tower
OX/KTN OX1 ....2 E5
School of St Helen &
St Katharine ABGD OX14 ....60 B2
Scotts House School &
Day Nursery RW/EYN OX29 ....12 D3
Sheldonian Theatre
OX/KTN OX1 ....3 F3
Shotover Country Park
HEAD OX3 ....36 A5
Somerville College
OXN/BOT/CM OX2 ....2 C1
Southfield Golf Club
COW/LTMR OX4 ....41 H1
South Oxford Health Centre
OX/KTN OX1 ....40 C3
Springfield School
WITNEY OX28 ....20 D2
Springfield Special School
WITNEY OX28 ....21 H1
Stanford University Centre
OX/KTN OX1 ....3 G4
Station Field Industrial Estate
KID OX5 ....9 G3
Summer Fields School
OXN/BOT/CM OX2 ....26 C4
Summertown Clinic
OXN/BOT/CM OX2 ....26 B4
Summertown Health Centre
OXN/BOT/CM OX2 ....26 B5
Sunningwell CE School
MCHM/KBPZ OX13 ....55 G1
Sunningwell School of Art
MCHM/KBPZ OX13 ....55 H1
Templars Retail Park
COW/LTMR OX4 ....42 A4
Temple Cowley County
Middle School
COW/LTMR OX4 ....42 A3
Temple Cowley Health Centre
COW/LTMR OX4 ....42 A4

Temple Cowley Pool
COW/LTMR OX4 ....42 A4
Templeton College
OX/KTN OX1 ....49 H1
Thameside Primary School
ABGD OX14 ....60 B5
Thames Valley Police
Headquarters KID OX5 ....17 H1
Thames View Business
Centre ABGD OX14 ....61 E3
Thomas Reade Primary
School ABGD OX14 ....61 F2
Tilsley Park Sports & Leisure
Centre ABGD OX14 ....55 H4
Tower Hill County Primary
School WITNEY OX28 ....20 D2
Training Standards Council
COW/LTMR OX4 ....42 B5
Travel Inn
ABGD OX14 ....60 A4
COW/LTMR OX4 ....42 C5
Travelodge
OXN/BOT/CM OX2 ....25 H1
WHLY OX33 ....45 G2
Trinity College
OX/KTN OX1 ....2 E2
Trinity College Sports Ground
HEAD OX3 ....34 B4
Two Rivers Industrial Estate
WITNEY OX28 ....21 F4
Ultimate Picture Palace
Cinema COW/LTMR OX4 ....3 K5
University College
OX/KTN OX1 ....3 F4
OXN/BOT/CM OX2 ....33 F1
University College Sports
Ground OX/KTN OX1 ....40 D3
University of Oxford
COW/LTMR OX4 ....41 F1
OX/KTN OX1 ....2 C3
OX/KTN OX1 ....2 D1
OX/KTN OX1 ....2 D2
OX/KTN OX1 ....3 G1
OX/KTN OX1 ....3 G2
OX/KTN OX1 ....3 G4
OX/KTN OX1 ....33 G3
OX/KTN OX1 ....33 G3
OX/KTN OX1 ....40 D4

OXN/BOT/CM OX2 ....2 A4
OXN/BOT/CM OX2 ....33 G2
University of Oxford
Botanic Garden OX/KTN OX1 ....3 G4
University Science Area
OX/KTN OX1 ....33 H3
The Upper Reaches Hotel
ABGD OX14 ....60 D4
Victoria Hotel
OX/KTN OX1 ....40 D3
Wadham College
OX/KTN OX1 ....3 F2
Warneford Hospital
HEAD OX3 ....34 D5
Wellbeing Clinic
OXN/BOT/CM OX2 ....33 E3
Wessex Industrial Estate
WITNEY OX28 ....21 F5
West End Industrial Estate
WITNEY OX28 ....21 F2
Westgate Shopping Centre
OX/KTN OX1 ....2 D4
West Kidlington Primary
School KID OX5 ....17 G1
West Oxford Health Centre
OXN/BOT/CM OX2 ....32 D5
West Oxford Primary School
OXN/BOT/CM OX2 ....32 D5
West Oxfordshire Technical
College WITNEY OX28 ....21 E3
West Way Health Centre
OX/KTN OX1 ....39 E1
West Witney County Primary
School WITNEY OX28 ....20 C3
Westwood Country Hotel
OX/KTN OX1 ....49 F2
Wheatley Business Centre
WHLY OX33 ....45 E1
Wheatley CE Primary School
WHLY OX33 ....44 B1
Wheatley Park School
WHLY OX33 ....37 H4
Wheatley Rugby Club
WHLY OX33 ....37 H4
White Horse Leisure &
Tennis Centre ABGD OX14 ....61 F3
William Fletcher Primary
School KID OX5 ....16 C3

Windale Primary School
COW/LTMR OX4 ....51 G3
Windmill Primary School
HEAD OX3 ....35 F4
Windrush Health Centre
WITNEY OX28 ....21 E2
Windrush Leisure Centre
WITNEY OX28 ....21 F3
Witney Community Hospital
WITNEY OX28 ....21 E3
Witney Museum
WITNEY OX28 ....21 F2
Wolfson College
OXN/BOT/CM OX2 ....33 G1
Wolvercote Cemetery
OXN/BOT/CM OX2 ....26 A1
Wolvercote First School
OXN/BOT/CM OX2 ....25 H3
Woodeaton Manor School
.................19 G3
Woodfarm Health Centre
HEAD OX3 ....42 C1
Wood Farm Primary School
HEAD OX3 ....35 F5
Wood Green School
WITNEY OX28 ....21 H2
Woodstock CE Primary
School WDSTK OX20 ....5 E4
Woodstock Swimming Pool
WDSTK OX20 ....5 F4
Woodstock Town Hall
WDSTK OX20 ....4 C4
Woolgate Shopping Centre
WITNEY OX28 ....21 F3
Wootton St Peters CE
Primary School
OX/KTN OX1 ....47 H4
Worcester College
OX/KTN OX1 ....2 C2
Wychwood School
OXN/BOT/CM OX2 ....33 G2
Wycliffe Hall
OXN/BOT/CM OX2 ....33 G3

Acknowledgements

Post Office is a registered trademark of Post Office Ltd. in the UK and other countries.

ools address data provided by Education Direct.

rol station information supplied by Johnsons

-way street data provided by © Tele Atlas N.V.   Tele Atlas

'den centre information provided by

'den Centre Association    Britains best garden centres

evale Garden Centres

Street by Street   QUESTIONNAIRE

Dear Atlas User
Your comments, opinions and recommendations are very important to us.
So please help us to improve our street atlases by taking a few minutes
to complete this simple questionnaire.

You do not need a stamp (unless posted outside the UK). If you do not want to remove this page from your street atlas, then photocopy it or write your answers on a plain sheet of paper.

Send to: The Editor, AA Street by Street, FREEPOST SCE 4598,
Basingstoke RG21 4GY

ABOUT THE ATLAS...

Which city/town/county did you buy?

Are there any features of the atlas or mapping that you find particularly useful?

Is there anything we could have done better?

Why did you choose an AA Street by Street atlas?

Did it meet your expectations?

Exceeded ☐   **Met all** ☐   **Met most** ☐   **Fell below** ☐

Please give your reasons

ML093z

continued overleaf

Where did you buy it?

For what purpose? (please tick all applicable)

To use in your own local area ☐   To use on business or at work ☐

Visiting a strange place ☐   In the car ☐   On foot ☐

Other (please state)

LOCAL KNOWLEDGE...

Local knowledge is invaluable. Whilst every attempt has been made to make the information contained in this atlas as accurate as possible, should you notice any inaccuracies, please detail them below (if necessary, use a blank piece of paper) or e-mail us at *streetbystreet@theAA.com*

ABOUT YOU...

Name (Mr/Mrs/Ms)

Address

Postcode

Daytime tel no

E-mail address

Which age group are you in?

Under 25 ☐   25-34 ☐   35-44 ☐   45-54 ☐   55-64 ☐   65+ ☐

Are you an AA member? YES ☐   NO ☐

Do you have Internet access? YES ☐   NO ☐

Thank you for taking the time to complete this questionnaire. Please send it to us as soon as possible, and remember, you do not need a stamp (unless posted outside the UK).

We may want to contact you about other products and services provided by us, or our partners (by mail, telephone) but please tick the box if you DO NOT wish to hear about such products and services from us by mail or telephone. ☐

ML093z